LIVERPOOL
IN A CITY LIVING 3
THE TENEMENTS

First Published 2006 by Countyvise Limited,
14 Appin Road, Birkenhead, Wirral CH41 9HH

British Library Cataloguing in Publication Data.
A catalogue record for this book is available from the British Library.

Please note: From 1st January 2007 ISBNs will contain 13 numbers. These numbers will be the same as the present number printed below the barcode (ie. starting 978). Countyvise is showing both existing (10 digit) and future (13 digit) ISBNs on the Title page verso. Please continue to use the 10 figure number until 31st December 2006.

ISBN: 1 901231 76 3 ISBN: 978 1 901231 76 2

Dedicated to my parents Norah and Joe with special thanks to my wife Ann and children Melanie, Melissa and Katy

INTRODUCTION

If we take conservative estimates that there were 50 developments of inter-war tenements in Liverpool each with an average of 200 flats. If we again take a conservative figure of 4 to a family with each family living for 10 years in these blocks, most of the blocks having a 50 year lifespan - we can see that around 40,000 people will have been living at any one time in this type of housing and that overall, around 200,000 people will have at one time or another climbed the stairwell, swept the yard, viewed from the landing or at least crossed the doorstep of one of these flats as a resident.

I was encouraged, after publication of my first two books which largely centred on the Gerard Gardens and Liverpool 3 area of the city, to widen the scope to include all of Liverpool's inter-war tenement blocks. I was constantly asked 'have you got pictures of this' or 'can you help me with that' and I discovered previously unseen and unpublished photographs from ex residents and ex pats alike which just had to be shared. There's no doubt that while the new housing with their central heating and gardens were lovely, the number of petitions and movements made by organisations to keep the old communities together means that the old tenement environment meant a lot to them.

Another reason behind it is there are many, many books concentrating on the marvellous civic buildings and unique architecture in the city. While these are fabulous in their own right, photographs of such, rehashed from a different angle or perspective can only be sustained for so long. I noticed while looking for photographs of where I grew up and lived that there weren't that many readily available or previously published. There was nothing on the social housing situation from the 1930s onwards and particularly the tenements and it was something I had to put right so here we are. Initially, it was just a joy to see Holly Street, Christian Street and Gerard Crescent in a book somewhere, it didn't really matter that I'd done it.

ALL PLAY AND NO WORK

(FOR US KIDS ANYWAY)

Having lived in three of the grandest Municipal tenement housing developments during my childhood, at a time of course which is impressionable, I feel well versed, as no doubt many are, to give an accurate account of what it was like growing up there. For the sake of this testimony, I use Gerard Crescent and Gerard Gardens, but I'm sure that the same could stand for almost all of the tenement blocks in Liverpool.

In fact my older brother, Joey, ended up living in another couple of these walk up flats, firstly up at Great Richmond Street, which still stand today and then at Vauxhall Gardens. Do you remember those blokes who used to walk around with the Bruce Springsteen and his E Street band tour dates on the back of their T-shirts. Well our Joey had one saying 'on tour' with a list of all the tenement blocks he lived in - no, only kidding.

As soon as I was deemed old enough to enter the foray into the 'square' below, the hive of activity soon became apparent. Only previously marvelled at from the top landing of our block, safe from the swerving bikes, whizzing footballs, swinging cricket bats and verbal banter. The crescendo of noise somehow seemed accentuated by the design of the high long landings which surrounded us.

It's true to say that before the advent of Nintendo's, Play stations and X boxes, we made our own playtime and the interactive games we played were with and against other human beings, not computer imagery - in the flesh as it were - but not literally of course - Ooh matron! Brainpower, adventure, speed of thought and battling became effortless in the never ending endeavours each weekend and evening after school. Bonding, solution finding, problem solving et al might be the language of the admin office of today, but these were things we did unknowingly, without a second thought on a day to day basis in the community spirited arena that was at the centre of our homes.

We'd play out all day and at night till it got dark, no one was able to reach us as mobile phones were in the future and about as likely in the early 70s as being beamed up by Scottie but no one minded. I'm sure there were as many paedophiles and murderers knocking around then as there are now but the media coverage of such or even perhaps the knowledge of them was negligible.

We rode the bikes of the day. The Chopper for instance with its 3 speed gear lever on the crossbar. I see the new version had that changed to the handlebar for safety reasons - What piffle! - That's the where there's blame there's a claim for you, something that didn't bother us back then. The Tomahawk was the other popular bike, the grifter coming later, though my mates and I preferred the good old racer with the narrowest of tyres. Cundles on Pembroke Place kept us well supplied with accessories like chequered handlebar tape, mileometers, rubber grips, stickers, lights, bell and a water bottle in its holder.

We'd go through phases. Sometimes one of us would have a steery, possibly made by one of our dads. That's a self propelled go-kart to anyone posh who is reading this. A crossed plank of wood on a pivot bolt with pram wheels and a rope to pull left or right for steering with. We'd drink from a shared bottle of pop, long before the experts would make a packet from hosting T.V. programmes telling us we shouldn't do this, but no one died.

Girls would play gutters or kerbies, standing each side of the road that ran around the inside of the square. This would entail throwing a ball at the topside corner of the kerb and getting the ball to rebound straight back to you where you caught it and scored a point each time you did so. If you didn't succeed, the ball would go straight to your opponent on the opposite side who would then try the same trick.
Another thing we'd do, requiring no equipment whatsoever, was dodging the cracks in the pavement as we walked along. Heaven forbid if you inadvertently stepped on one, as the punishment would be that you'd 'go out' with Mary Kill the cat or Mary Herbert - female undesirables in the area - weren't we cruel. The girls were no less afflicted - their punishment for any of their misdemeanours would result in them having to wed Kenny kick the can - often heard in the backies - which was obviously just the wind blowing a can, even if it

was uphill which added to the strange phenomenon. Another trick was to walk along the kerbside as though it was a tightrope, often falling all of three inches into the gutter to the screams of aaaarrrrgh.

Another pastime was hopscotch, an old Victorian street game whereby grids would be marked out on the pavement with chalk. A stone would be thrown into numbered squares, the first player starting with the first square. You'd have to hop over that square landing on the next with two feet. If two squares were side by side, you'd land with a foot in each. At the top end of the grid, you'd turn and hopscotch back down stopping at the square where the stone was, lean over, pick up the stone and hop onto that square. Once completed the next player would do the very same. The first player would move onto the next number and so on but if your stone missed the intended square or you stood on a line or put both feet down when you're supposed to be hopping then your opponent gets a go and you have to repeat your failed number the next time it was your turn.

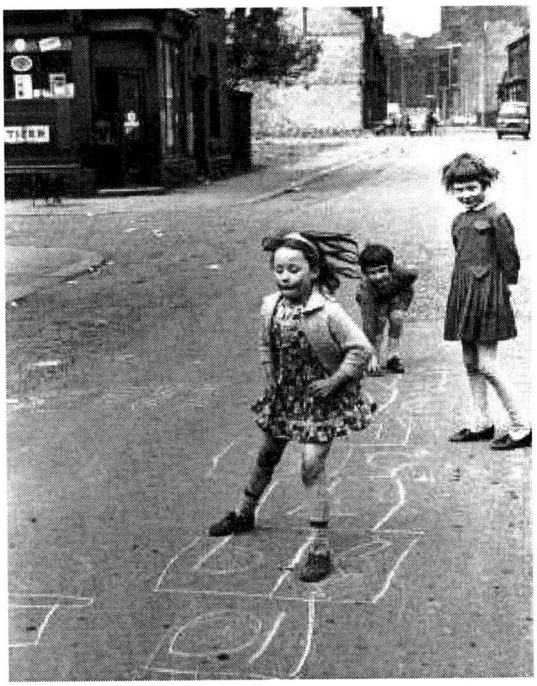

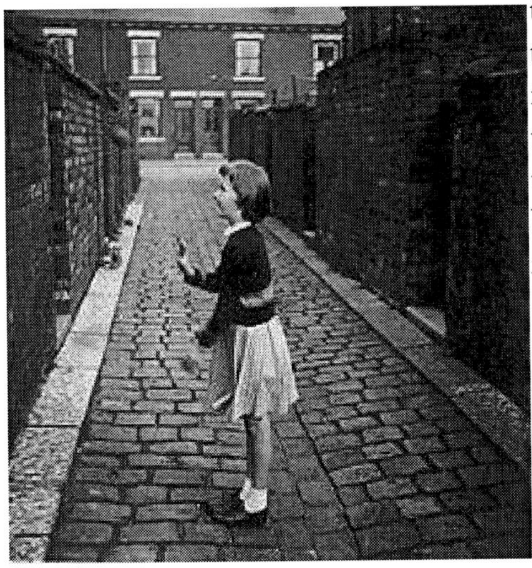

The girls of the tennies would also play two balls against any available wall, usually the one on the stairwell at the end of the landing. Legs akimbo and skirts tucking into their knickers, they would whizz a couple of tennis balls against the wall in juggler fashion and throw the balls through their legs from behind them, rebounding them off the concrete floor onto the wall at such a speed they would become a blur whilst reciting a mantra that didn't make sense to any of us passing lads who would usually try to put them off mid-stream.

Another mesmerising activity of theirs with equal speed of hand was skipping. This could be done singularly or where two girls would swish a rope around at breakneck speed as another girl jumped in (that alone would floor us lads). Again, songs would accompany the activity.

'I can do the baseball, I can do the splits. I can do the twirly whirly, I can do the kicks.
The Queens she bows, the King salutes, the girls show their knickers, the boys blow the kisses, and they all shout salami, salami all the boys are barmy - sss'late, sss'late - all the girls are great'

'I call in my very best friend (say their name until they jump in the rope with you)
Sandra likes coffee, Sandra likes tea, Sandra likes sitting on her boyfriends knee.....'

To the tune of the Liver Birds sitcom...

'On the mountain stands a lady, who she is I do not know,
All she wants is gold and silver *(don't they all)* - all she wants is a nice young beau,
So call in my very best friend, very best friend, my very best friend,
Call in my very best friend while I go out to play' (then their very best friend would jump in. While they jumped out)

Other mantra's included 'salt, mustard, vinegar, pepper' which increased in tempo whilst skipping as well as 'Jelly on a plate, jelly on a plate, wibble wobble, wibble wobble, jelly on a plate.' -and the last one ....

'The big ship sails through the alley alley oh, the alley alley oh, the alley alley oh,
The big ship sails through the alley alley oh on the last day of September.'

Hoola hoops were also the craze for a while. Brightly coloured hoops of plastic would be rotated round and round the body by the gentle swaying of hips. Those that were really good at it could do a few at once. I bet some lads would have a go of their sister's one on the sly, perhaps in the privacy of their bedroom - you know who you are - and before you start, I didn't have any sisters.

If both your parents were working, you might've been afforded a space hopper, one of the top toys of the early 1970s. Usually of an orange brown colour, part of the fun was avoiding the glass particles and sharp stones on your trek around the square. Black patches from your brother's cycle puncture repair outfit would take the look off it really.

Football matches in the square went on until the first team to score twenty or because of bad light stopping play with 'the next goal the winner'. The teams would usually consist of one square or block of residents against another, usually their closest 'rivals'. It could get quite cramped at times with fifteen aside in half the space of a proper footy pitch. Jumpers would form the goalposts, sometimes the pole from the squares standard lamp would be used as one of the posts. One problem though was no crossbar and this would result in arguments about whether it was a goal or not.

Obstacles to contend with would include the bonfire damaged centre circle with such delights as splintered glass and gravel which created more slide tackles and cut knees and elbows than were intended - Ouch - get out the Dettol and Germoline. Sometimes the kerb would actually beat you as you homed in on goal and if the ball ever went into one of the rubbish chute outlets in between the yards of the ground floor flats, there would be a free for all, still got a scab on my left ankle now.

If only four or five friends were playing out, the football game would take the form of what we called '60 seconds'. Using one of the staircase entrances as a goal, turns would be taken in goal - you'd have to be fast off the mark and shout 'last goalie' then someone would shout 'second to last' etc, as you could end up in there a long time. The object was for the outfield players to join forces and keep the goalie in by scoring headers past him. The goalie would count loudly to 60 but each time a goal was scored, he'd have to start again from the beginning. Volleys could be scored once the goalie reached 40 in his counting and as he got near the end of his stint, the seconds would inevitably get faster and louder in pleasurable anticipation of getting out of goal before one of the volleys crashed in off his head at 70mph, Peter Lorimer style.

Should there be up to a dozen lads up for a game of footy which is not enough for a full blown match, a game of 'pairs' would be arranged. Numbers would be chosen for each player and the goalie, who wouldn't be privy to them would shout them out so that for instance, number 6 might be paired with number 2 and number 4 may be paired with number 1 etc. A knockout game would ensue with usually the first round being decided by just a single goal and you were through to the next round until only two pairs were left in the final and that game may be decided by two or three goals.

Another popular game of footy for when there were only a few of us was 'Hit the post' or 'Spot'. This would entail us taking turn to piece in trying to hit the pole in the square which was the lighting pole that was used as one of the goalposts in the full blown matches. In each round, the person to hit the pole the least was out. The remaining players would then battle it out until only two were left in the final.

Open gates is a game remembered by the slightly older crew. The idea here would be to get from one side of the 'square' to the other without getting 'ticked' by whoever was 'man' in the middle. Similar to British Bulldogs, if ticked, you went on their side to try and stop the rest. Upon reaching the other side you could shout open gates but the twist being that you didn't take your own name so when someone called 'you' to make the run, it would be made by someone else who'd borrowed your name for the game and you'd have someone elses.

Summer would see the cobwebs blown from the cricket bat. With the most basic of equipment that would consist of one leg pad for each batsman, a wicket would be chalked onto a suitable wall, the one in Gerard Crescent being the end of the wall that stopped at the top of the brow in front of Thurlow House. The trouble with painted or chalked wickets were the constant arguments about whether you were bowled out or not. And so with progress came the bread crate wickets, duly nicked from the back of the Sunblest wagon delivering to Jim Moran's grocers shop.

The crate would be somewhat larger than the average set of wickets and so it was easier for the bowler. Should you make contact with the ball though, there were certain rules. If you smacked the ball, hitting the face of the landings opposite, it was a straight 6 automatically without having to run. If you were unlucky enough that the ball actually landed on a landing and didn't come back down - it was 6 and out and to rub salt in the wounds, you'd have to run up the stairs to retrieve the ball unless someone was passing.

A 4 was scored if you hit any of the surrounding yards at ground level, again as long as the ball didn't enter and stay in the yard and so on. If you skimmed the ball behind you which usually resulted in the ball proceeding to roll down the brow to the collective tune from the outfielders of 'well, I'm not going for it' - you were out. This did away with the need for a wicket keeper. If you hit one of the Millers on the head, serving in their nearby 'mobile' in the square - it was time to run - but in the opposite direction.

Bonfire night and in particular the build up to it sticks fondly in the memory. With living on the top landing, end house, there would always be activity in the immediate run up to 'bommy night'. Doors would be passed up to the flat bit of roof above the stairwell for safe keeping. Precariously positioned in the blustery November night would be a couple of the bravest lads, stacking up the night's plunder, away from the prying eyes of would be thieves from other blocks. First though would be the short journey over to the disused breweries and warehouses of the surrounding area. Across Byrom Street was out of bounds as that was Fonney Oy territory and the thought of a split lip whilst chapped during the winter months wasn't too pleasant.

Gangs of kids would make their way back from the bombdies to the sanctuary of their square. A straight line, just like an army of worker ants, hidden under the doors they were carrying. When safe storage spots were full, the remainder of the booty had to be guarded with life and limb. On the night itself, just after tea-time, doors, cabinets, crates, pallets and anything that would burn and even some things that wouldn't, were sent drifting down into the square from the landings. Chairs would be stacked, the obligatory mattress would take pride of place amongst the wigwam shaped cone in the centre of the square.

The prayers for a dry night would usually go unanswered as the bonfire got under way. In no time at all the flames would be reaching above the lower landings with the sparks flying high up into the night sky, the crackling sound still in my head as though it were yesterday. There would be a gathering of locals who would move from square to square to see how their rivals were getting on with theirs - the inevitable 'ours is bigger than that' would ring out to replies of 'no way'. I can remember on more than one occasion being amongst the last of the remaining few, poking away at the dying embers to try and keep the fire going as others larked about trying to throw each other onto the orange glowing remains. Next day - only 364 to go.

Every now and then, a local parish priest or a self organised party of mothers would arrange for a charabanc day trip out to Southport, Blackpool or Wales. These would include a bagged 'sarnie' lunch which would be warm and squelchy by the time your rumbling belly would inform you it was time to eat. Colomendy/Loggerheads was a favourite of many as well as the beaches of North Wales. A police escort was given on one occasion as the kids were run out of town with a 'don't come back' retort ringing in the ears - Prestatyn had never seen the likes of it, but a few John Wayne films had.

My own memories were of my mam and dad taking me, and sometimes my friends on the Royal Daffodil when it used to berth at New Brighton pier. The pier contained the ghost train and we used to have a great time at the resort on our doorstep but sadly I am too young to remember the figure of 8 or the tower. We'd be allowed down to the rocks if the tide was out, catching crabs by lifting up the stones and finding them hiding in the nooks and crannies but you had to be careful not to slip on the mossy sandstone formations. You'd bring a few home in a plastic bucket, flicking the water at them intermittently to carefully keep them alive, as if that ever did any good. Your bedroom would reek like New Brighton and the Mersey for days. A few days later, you'd awake for school to be greeted by your last Mr Crab floating on his back. That dinner time my mam would serve me a crab paste buttie - I'd make her show me the Princes jar first though.

The bus ride to Crosby on the Ribble L3 from Skelhorne Street depot seemed like hundreds of miles away back then. The sand dunes at Crosby before the Marina was built went right back to the big white houses on the front. There were those concrete pyramids in the sand at the shore, designed to stop tanks landing from craft during the war. At other times my dad would take us on the 59 to the Old Roan depot where the row of shops facing on Aintree Lane would furnish us with fishing nets and sweets. We'd proceed to the nearby Liverpool/Leeds canal to hunt down the stickleback which were usually too fast for us. A great day out though nevertheless.

Weekends would be spent traipsing around the Walker Art Gallery and Museum. Living just 5 minutes away, that was easy for us. We'd be on the 'snifter' for girls and would bashfully follow some around for what seemed like hours on end. Playing games with us they'd rush to another floor giggling, where we'd eventually stumble across them again as we turned a corner - to much embarrassment to us all - can't remember that we actually ever spoke to any of them. In doing so though, we got to know every painting and exhibit on show - every room like the back of our hand - every attendant.

The Museum for instance had that old cobbled street where you could press the button to sounds of children playing and singing Ring o' ring o' Roses - the song from the times of the great plague. Then there was that big glass case with the pinewoods, railway and coastline of Freshfield and Ainsdale in it. You'd press a button and a little light would come on in the middle of the forest with a caption telling you what and where it was.

The basement had the 'Rocket' locomotive, the old fire engine and the first Ford Anglia to come off the Halewood production line - a pale green one, which eventually found its way into the Museum of Liverpool Life at Mann Island. The old aquarium with tanks either side of that dark long passageway was much better than the current one too. At the staircase end were other glass tanks with lizards, snakes, stick insects and tarantulas in them - you see - I was paying attention.

Evenings would sometimes see us hang around by the Steble fountain in William Brown Street, just a stones throw from the square. We would play football tick on the three giant steps of the Wellington Column whereby whoever was man would have to kick the ball up from ground level at those on the steps. Ordinary tick was also played on these steps at a frenetic pace, it's a wonder no-one ever went ass over tit and it would have been a long fall, have you seen how high those steps are? Sometimes we'd even play shooties in the subway itself, if there were three of us it would be one and off, winner stays on. The pain, was having to wait while people passed through, I mean, couldn't they have used the traffic lights?

Hide n' seek down in St. John's Gardens was another favourite with the dozens of statues to hide behind or laying low in the sunken flower beds, though we never wantonly damaged the flowers, that wasn't part of the game. Still, the cocky watchman didn't see it that way and would come out of his den, built into the stone wall under the steps. Sometimes, the little parks and gardens van would come round and chase us out, we'd give cheek while legging it but it never went any further than that. Other variations of Hide n' seek, usually played in and around the square were 'Kick the can' and Allallio - in both games the last one in saved all if he made it back to den or kicked the can ahead of whoever was 'man', this meant that everyone who was captured were released.

It's often said, sometimes through rose tinted glasses that those were the good old days when doors could be left open, people were 'House proud' even though it was only flats we lived in but I did honestly see all of that. Many relatives and good friends going back years lived in our tenements and New Years Eve was always a 'gas'.
People would go from door to door along the landing, wishing everyone all the best, while popping in for a Harvey's Bristol cream - usually a couple of families somewhere on the block would be having a party with open doors. It was here I tasted my first beer from a big giant Watney's party 7 can. In fact the bloke I sneaked it from used to take one to the match, drink it on the way then stand on the empty so he could see better.

The mothers, or their daughters would get the white paint out now and then and go along the landing with a strip of white paint, even carefully going around the drainpipes and grids. If there was a wedding on the block, a May procession, or if it was First Holy Communion time or a Parish priest cavalcade, this would be extended to the staircase too. No one wanted to be shown up.

There were hardly any cars in the square in the early 1970s, in fact it was a novelty for anyone to have a telephone. There was no 'school run'. Grosvenor Street or Fontenoy Street were not chocker block with 4 x 4's that had come from only half a mile away. We, as kids actually walked to school. It was part of the fun, a lark along the way, especially in the winter if it had been snowing, wearing our coats only by the hood. It was a different story in the night time though. The blue snorkel parka with bright orange lining was all the fashion.

Making our own entertainment in the evening, sometimes just even gathering on the stairs of the block to gab could be a freezing pastime. The hood would be pulled up and out, it was like looking through a periscope. Around this time you could walk through St. John's precinct at night, window shopping. We'd see all the 'smellies' heading down to the 'Moonstone' pub on their rock night out. There were actually 6 pubs built into St. John's at this time. The Star and Garter, The Penny Farthing, The Sportsman, The Cunarder and The Moonstone as well as the Top Rank club upstairs which became Romeo and Juliets.

The lads and I had a mad idea of going camping so we'd check out the windows of the famous Army stores and Millets before popping into the Blessed Sacrament Holy Shrine in Clayton Square for a warm after lighting a candle. This was also around the time of the 'Suss - stop and search law' so we'd always be getting stopped by the Police asking what we were up to. The honest answer was nothing - we just lived so nearby and were bored rigid, this was our playground, our adventure.

I remember The Shakespeare Theatre going up in flames in Fraser Street, 1976 it was, all rushing over there and watching the firemen tackle the blaze. That area was awash with picture houses and theatres. The Shaky, The Paramount, The Odeon, The Gaumont, The Empire. The blaze at St. Johns too - the rumours about it starting in 'Habitat' still fresh in the mind. Watching the Orange Lodge march down London Road to the St. George's Hall, it was just a band to us. A gang of lads racing down, saying there'd been trouble along Netherfield Road and my mam telling me in later years to stay away from the 'Tugboat' pub (which we frequented) on the 12th July - we never did stay away, it was alright we knew everyone. Thankfully, that sort of bigotry in Liverpool seems to have stopped.

GARDENS OF STONE
BY PAUL SUDBURY

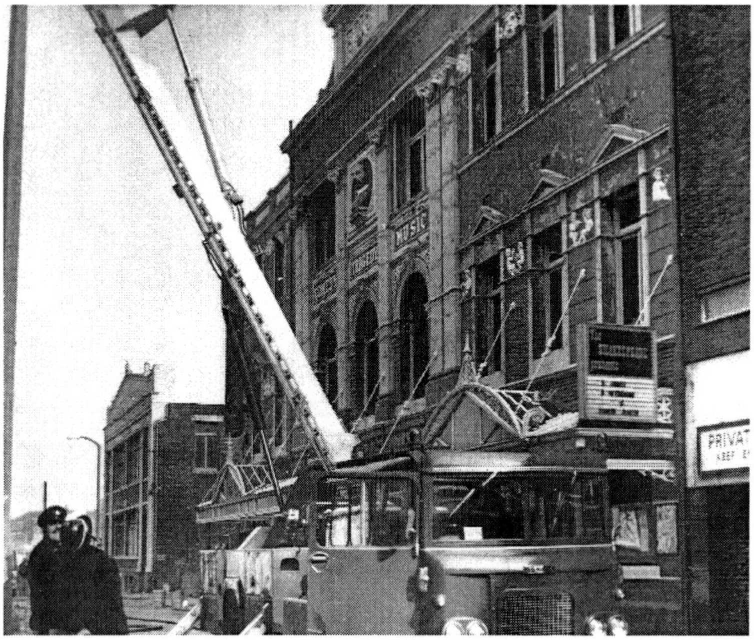

The Morning after the big blaze. A Simon Snorkel still in attendance damping down at the Shakespeare Theatre 1976. Comedy Tragedy Music says the well known phrase under the bust of William himself. The Paramount Picture House to its left is still there now as the Bar De Mille.

In the gardens of stone, I was sown.
Brought up by the sounds, of people I've known
I saw the face of fear, then saw it disappear, in the gardens of stone.

In the gardens of stone, I had grown.
Some stayed until the end, others had flown
I saw the eye of tear, then saw it disappear, in the gardens of stone.

In the gardens of stone, I was known.
A cinematic dream, a crane driver's son
I saw him come so near, then saw him disappear, in the gardens of stone.

In the gardens of stone, I was alone. A violent playground past, the final whistle blown.
I saw it all so clear, then saw it disappear, in the gardens of stone.

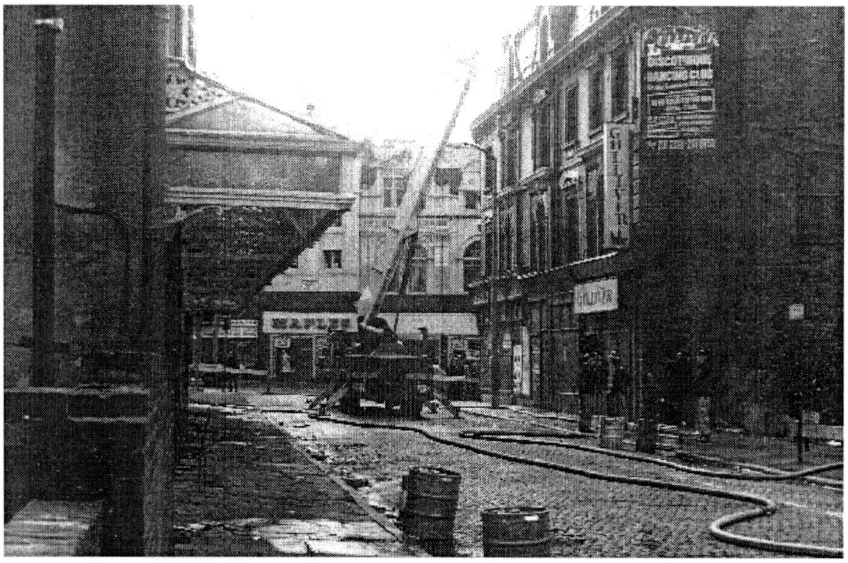

Looking along Fraser Street past Gullivers Discotheque towards London Road. Ann Fowler House Salvation Army building now occupies the Shakespeare Theatre site

INFLUENTIAL FIGURES IN THE IMPROVEMENT OF SANITATION AND HOUSING IN LIVERPOOL

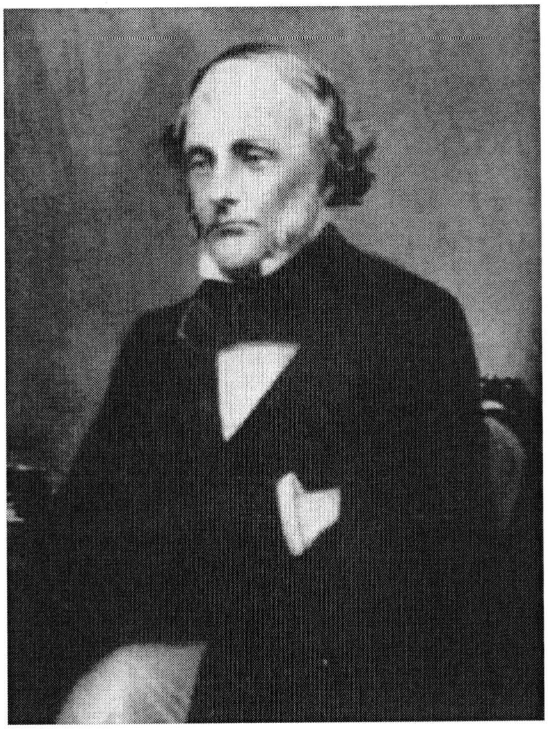

Dr. William Henry Duncan.

Born Liverpool 1805:

Born in Seel Street, he became Britain's first medical officer, assigned to Liverpool, helping to create the first sanitary act in 1846. He took up his role as Medical Officer of Health on New Year's Day the following year. Even so, Britain's first public wash-house and baths had been established on Upper Frederick Street some 5 years earlier, influenced and pioneered by Kitty Wilkinson. He recognised that there was a clear link between damp, unventilated overcrowded unsanitary housing with no clean running water and the outbreak of disease such as cholera, smallpox and typhus. His findings were to clear the path for acts to be passed and something to be done about these issues. He recorded that 25% of his patients lived in cellar property with up to 30 individuals living in an airless room. He died in 1863.

James Newlands.

Born Edinburgh 1813:

Appointed as Britain's first borough engineer for Liverpool in 1847 to work alongside Dr. Duncan, he paved the way for municipal engineering as we know it today. He engineered the world's earliest integrated sewerage system in Liverpool, the significance of which cannot be overrated.

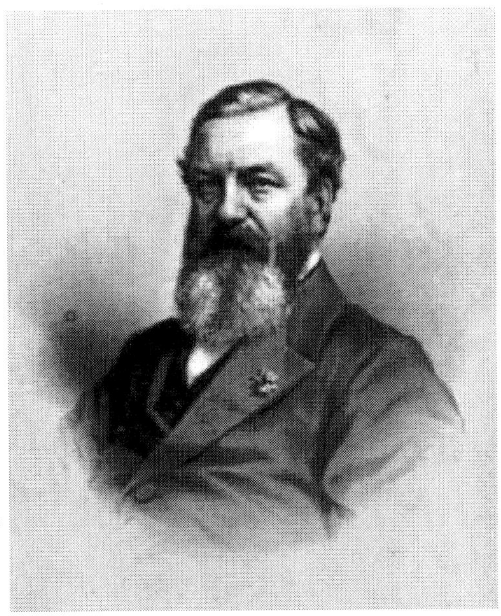

Implementing new building regulations, he was also responsible for effecting provision for public parks, and an efficient refuse collection service and street cleaning. He fought hard to get clean drinking water to the masses and brought in public bathing facilities. He succeeded in doubling the average life expectancy whilst in office from just 19 to 38. It was his idea to build a circular boulevard around the edge of the city as early as 1853 which was not to be realised until 50 years later under the direction of John Brodie. He died in 1871.

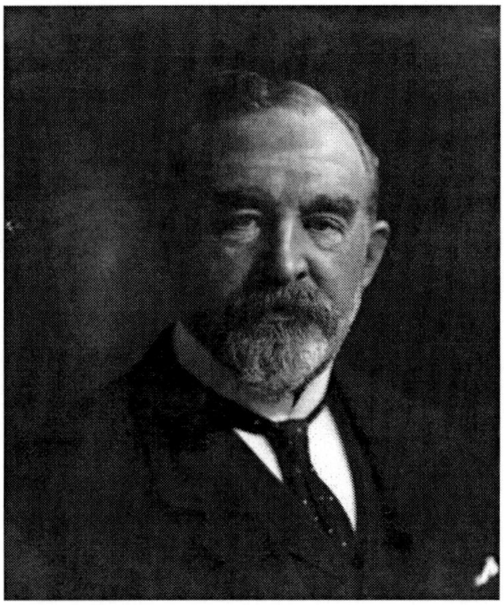

John Alexander Brodie.

Born Liverpool 1858:

Having plied his trade as a dock estate engineer at Liverpool from as young as 17 under the direction of one of Liverpool's great dock builders George Fosbery Lyster, successor to Jesse Hartley, he was appointed Liverpool city engineer in 1898. Brodie was one of the first to suggest the installation of an electric tram system in Liverpool, implementing the use of a central reservation for use by trams, the first stretch being from Edge Lane to Broadgreen in 1914. Within just 5 years of taking up his position, he had started to realise James Newland's vision of the city's ring road that was to be Queens Drive.

Creating a tree lined, grass verged boulevard with drinking fountains at regular intervals, a frontage fee would be charged to developers who wanted to build housing along its length, therefore it would become self financing. It was a mammoth task only completed in 1927, other major roads such as the East Lancs, Edge Lane Drive and Menlove Avenue were also proposed during this time and subsequently laid out from 1928.

Never to let the grass grow under his feet, Brodie also designed and built the first large panel reinforced prefabricated concrete housing in Britain, these being in Eldon Street, off Vauxhall Road in 1905. An exhibition of such undertaken in Letchworth was reported in the worldwide press, the technique influencing New York architect Grosvenor Atterbury in particular. Brodie's town planning skills were recognised internationally when in 1912 he was invited to India to help select a site and plan the new capital of India at Delhi. This culminated in attending the opening ceremony there in 1931.

In recognition of his many achievements including part planning of the world's largest underwater road tunnel, then being undertaken in Liverpool, he became the first local authority engineer to become president of the Institute of Civil Engineering. He was also President of the Liverpool Engineering Society and Associate Professor of Engineering at Liverpool University as well as being the Vice President of the Liverpool Self Propelled Traffic Association which went on to become the Royal Automobile Association (RAC). As an aside, he also somehow found the time to invent the football goal net back in 1890. He died in 1934.

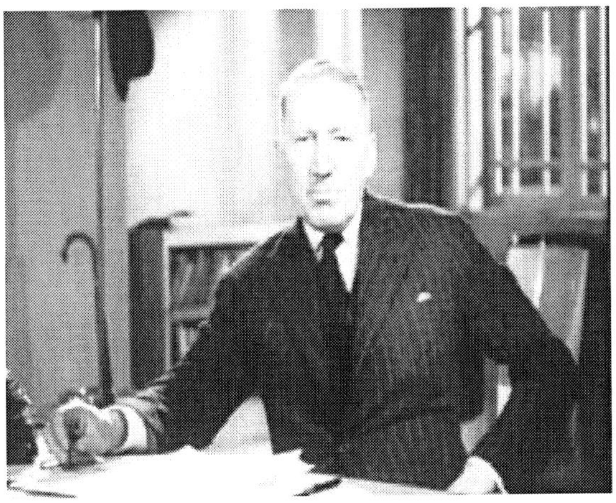

Lancelot Herman Keay

Born Eastbourne, Sussex 1883:

As successor to Brodie, one of his first jobs in office after being appointed City Architect and Director of Housing for Liverpool in 1925 was to oversee the Mersey Tunnel excavations and development. Closer to his heart though was his desire to undertake a mass slum clearance programme which would rid the city, and in particular its centre, of its most squalid unsanitary slums, courts and cellar property that were still in existence.

This involved compulsory purchase orders being placed on properties that were deemed unfit for habitation. Once the ownership of the said properties was transferred to the City Housing Department, demolition contractors could be brought in to raze them to the ground. Many town planning and housing acts were introduced after the first world war. Keay's vision was for whole new townships to spring up under his directorship. In August 1933 Lancelot Keay suggested that 5000 new houses should be built on the outskirts of the city and that 10,692 new flats should be constructed on the sites where slums had been cleared in the central area of the city. This was to be a ten year programme and in all Keay was responsible for more than 35,000 new houses and flats whilst in office.

Recognised for his flair and innovation in housing development, some of his most notable achievements were the creations of the township of Speke and the development of Norris Green. Speke became a model for self contained municipal housing estates throughout the world. Keay realised that it was important for shops, clothes washing facilities, children's playgrounds and libraries to be incorporated into his developments, something which was far seeing for that time.

During WWII it became difficult to get food which was rationed. In September 1940, Lord Woolton, The Minister of Food, himself from Liverpool, asked Keay to draw up plans for what were to become known as British Restaurants of which 2000 were to open across the land. The idea was that affordable food could be supplied to the general public whilst saving on fuel and power, thus preventing the need for these scarce commodities to be used at home.
On 11th November 1940 Lord Woolton opened Keay's first British Restaurant called 'Byrom' in Byrom Street, integrated into part of the Fontenoy Gardens re-housing scheme The second, called 'Myrtle' was opened by the Lord Mayor of Liverpool in Falkner Street on 3rd March 1941, again as part of a tenement block, this time Myrtle Gardens. In fact four of the first six British Restaurants were contained in tenement developments, the other two being in Warwick Gardens and Prince Albert Gardens. Air raid shelters were also built in the main squares of all of these housing schemes. After the war, Keay was responsible for earmarking suitable sites for the positioning of 'Prefabs' which were the temporary housing solution for the shortage of such due to the blitz.

Lancelot Keay became a Sir when he was knighted in 1947 for his contribution to public housing, serving as Director of Housing until the following year. He was also President of the Royal Institute of British Architects from 1946 to 1948. He died in 1974.

THE INTER-WAR TENEMENTS

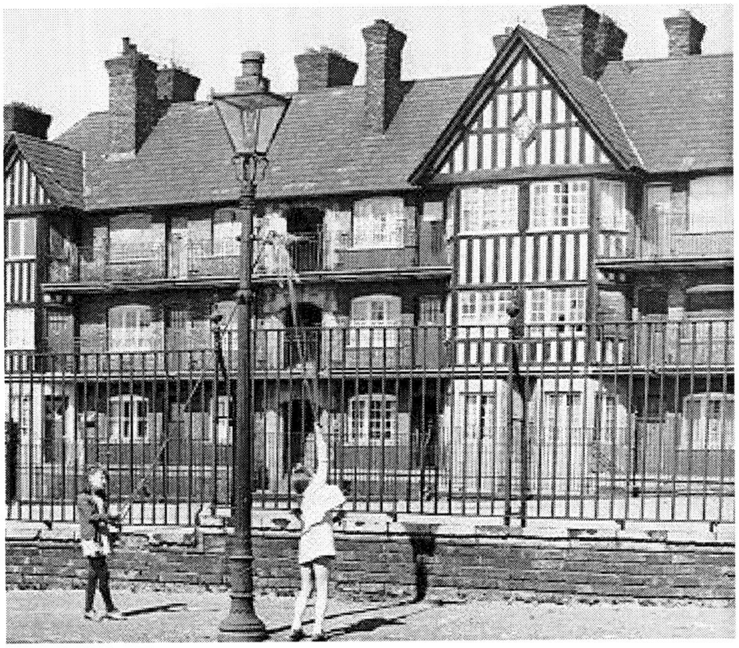

Eldon Grove in the Vauxhall area of the city.

Liverpool Corporation had already created a stock of labourers' landing dwellings prior to the First World War. This was largely of the type, one of which is still in existence in Eldon Grove, Vauxhall, Liverpool 3.

The Housing Acts of the 1930s were to see a vast improvement scheme, particularly in the central area of the city where much of the worst overcrowding in unsanitary property existed.

John Hughes and Gordon Stevenson were brought in as part of Lancelot Keay's design team, Keay being the City Architect and Housing Director under whose leadership the new Art Deco ultra modern developments were to be built.

To look at the earlier aforementioned buildings from the turn of the century to 1914 with their wrought iron railing landings, you would think that the new design was just a natural progression. Indeed the first inter-war tenements of the 1920s did contain railing landings but if we look in more detail as to what followed you would find that there was a definite shift away from the uniformity of the straight blocks of three high terraces and this was in some part due to a European influence.

In 1930, Liverpool Corporation sent housing representatives, under the direction of Lancelot Keay to the Dobling district of Vienna in Austria to study the Karl-Marx-Hof flats which were designed by their town planner, Karl Ehn, a follower of Otto Wagner. Built on land that until the 12th Century was under the waters of the Danube deep enough for ships to sail, the remaining pool was drained in 1750 by Holy Roman Emperor, Joseph II. Gardens were then built in the area which themselves were removed in the 1920s to make way for these flats.

The Social Democrats having gained control of the municipal administration during Austria's first republic (1918-1934) set about a programme of improving living conditions for the working class. The flats were to be assigned on the basis of a points system favouring families and the less affluent citizens. Typically, inter-war Gemeindebauten (German for Municipal Buildings) had a main arched entrance where one could enter into a large courtyard lined with trees and some greenery where children could play without having to go out onto the street. The flats themselves would be accessed from within.

Karl-Marx-Hof were built between 1927 and 1930 holding 1382 flats and was called the Ringstrasse des Proletariats or the Ring Street of the Proletariat. The development included many amenities such as a Laundromat, baths, Kindergarten, library, doctors offices and business section. The fortress like structure made the buildings adaptable for military use and during the Februaraufstand (February uprising) of the 1934 Osterreichischer Burgerkrieg (Austrian Civil war) those of the Social Democratic party who were engaged in the revolt barricaded themselves inside the Karl-Marx-Hof but were forced to surrender after the Austrian military of the Dollfuss, Red Army and the Austrofascist paramilitary bombarded them with artillery. At this point they renamed the flats Heiligenstadter Hof. They took their original name back in 1945 after WWII and the heavy artillery damage was repaired in the 1950s. The whole development was refurbished between 1989 and 1992.

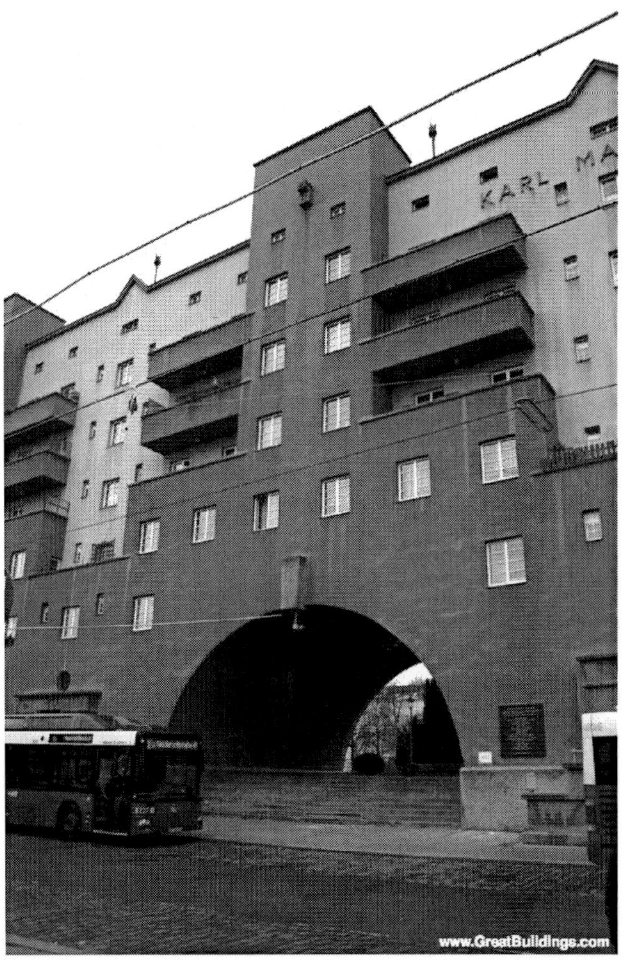

The Karl-Marx-Hof flats.

Lancelot Keay was a known fan of the Britz Horseshoe Estate that was commenced in 1925 in the NeuKoln district of Berlin, East Germany. These were designed by Bruno Taut and Martin Wagner. Built in seven phases of construction up until 1933, there were over 1000 flats on four floors. To avoid monotony, individual blocks were set forward or back as appropriate and spaces were left in between them at regular intervals forming a plaza. The buildings were set in symmetrical rows and varied in finishing materials and colour.

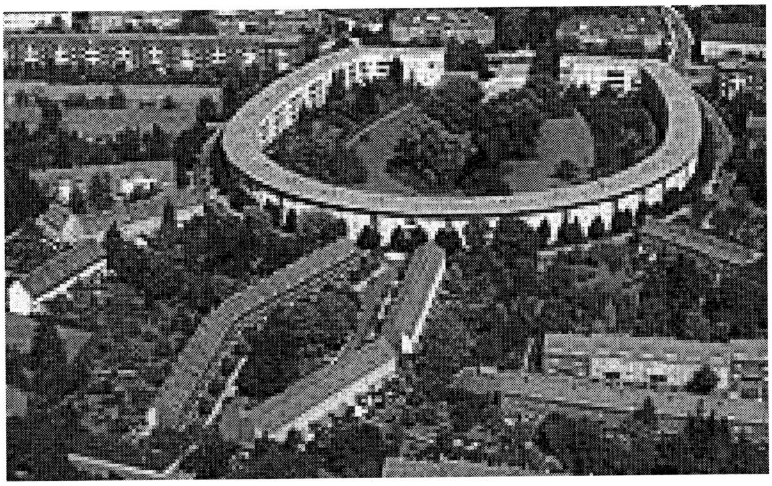

The Britz Horseshoe Estate.

Although their history is not as colourful as the Karl-Marx-Hof flats and they took longer to complete, the fact is they were a proto-type that influenced the later developments which can be seen in the Liverpool tenements that came a couple of years later.

It is clear that most of the designs in these two buildings were carried into what would become the largest building programme in Liverpool since the turn of the 20th Century. The large arched entrances would appear in buildings such as Gerard Gardens, Portland Gardens, Fontenoy Gardens and St. Andrews Gardens. The horseshoe shape itself would materialise in St. Andrews Gardens, known as the Bullring. Laundry and pressing facilities were sited in the Myrtle Gardens flats as well as a rest home at Caryl Gardens. Accommodation best suited for the elderly would be adjoined to the Brunswick Gardens and Speke Road Gardens developments and shrubs and greenery took pride of place in the likes of Wavertree Gardens and South Hill House.

Although a number of blocks housed an integral grocers shop, some, such as those on Soho Street, Fontenoy Gardens and St. Oswalds House' actually featured a row of retail premises beneath. More importantly in a family based, crowded community environment, nearly all of the Liverpool tenements had a central children's playground. Sculptures that were evident above the main arch of the Karl-Marx-Hof flats would materialise in the form of a hod carrier and Keay himself above the arches of Gerard Gardens.

However, it is also true that some of the European design didn't take a hold. The original drawings of the Liverpool tenements, housed in the Records Office suggest the architect's vision was to use plain white surfaces and a flat roof, as in the Britz Estate. A shortage of local plasterers meant that the design was modified to run with exposed brickwork. Having said that, where possible, parts of a few blocks had the monotony broken with sections of white rendered exteriors as seen in Caryl Gardens and Speke Road Gardens.

The Art Deco era had just seen the then tallest building in the world constructed in the USA in 1930, the impressive Empire State Building. Closer to home, Herbert J. Rowse was implementing this style of architecture as early as the 1920s. India Buildings (1923), The Queensway tunnel facia, ancillary buildings and George's Dock building ventilation shaft (1925), Martins Bank building, Water Street (1927) and the new Philharmonic Hall (1933) are all his works of art. Other notable Art Deco landmarks throughout the city during this period are Blackburn Assurance Buildings and the Ship and Mitre Public House which are both on Dale Street and further afield, the old Littlewoods Pools Building on Edge Lane and the original Speke Airport terminal.

NORTH OF THE CITY CENTRE.

MELROSE ROAD - KIRKDALE

In October 1925, plans were drawn up for the siting of four block complexes to the south side of Melrose Road, Kirkdale, Liverpool 4. With the township of Bootle just a few hundred yards along Stanley Road, these were to be the northern most inter-war tenement flats in Liverpool. The site of the former Owens saw mill and timber yard which was bordered by Owen, St.Agnes and Fonthill Road were cleared to make way for what were to become known locally as 'The Buildings'. Formally called Owen, Melrose, Fonthill and Stanley House, to the local children they were called 'the billogs'. They also christened the nearby recreation ground on the site of the old Kirkdale Gaol, 'the rec' and the railway sidings across Melrose Road became 'the raller'. Families started moving in around 1928, a great area of luxury was created for a part of Liverpool that was growing due to the close proximity of the docks and surrounding industrial premises. Of the earlier railing landings style, they contained over 400 flats, one block even housing an ornate clock.

They were demolished in 1983, new housing now standing on the newly created Tolpuddle and Poplar Way.

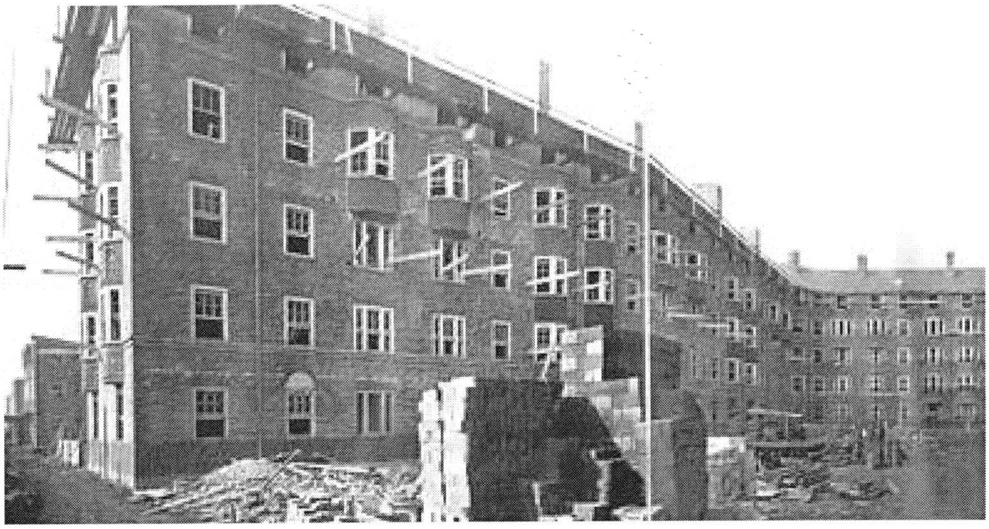

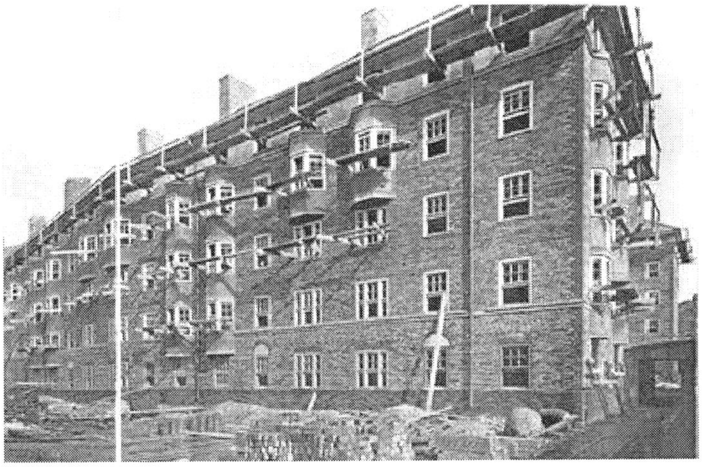

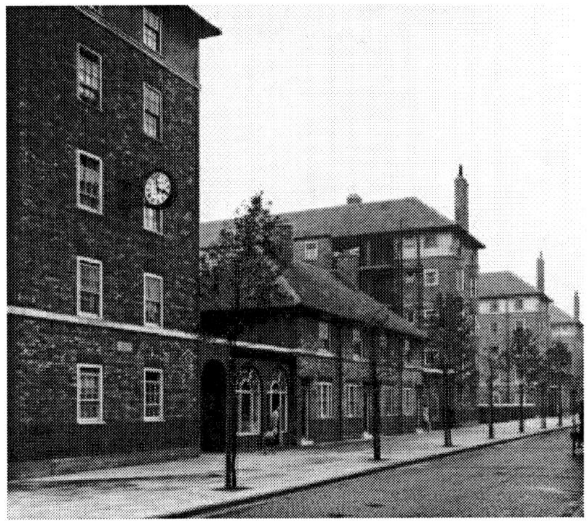

Owen House under construction in the 1920s and the finished Fonthill block from the front and a view of the clock from Owen Road.

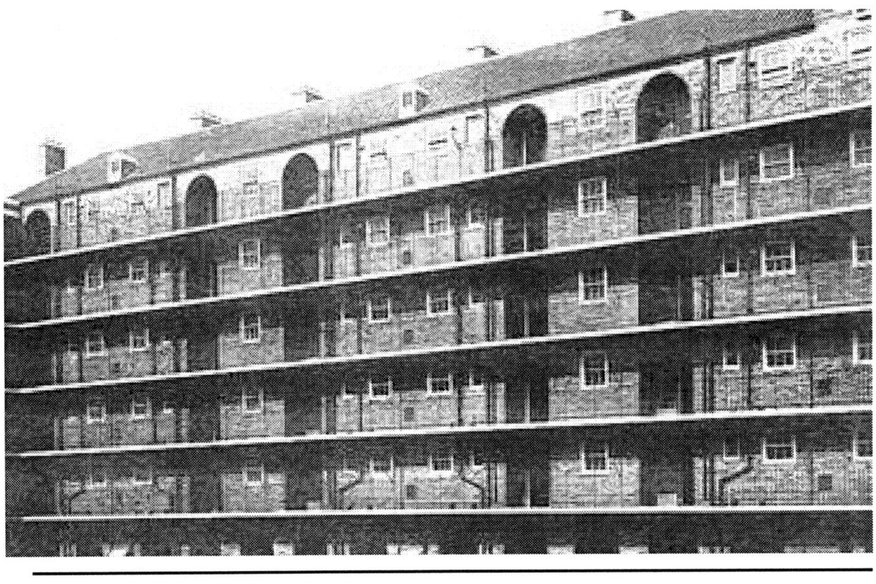

ST. DOMINGO ROAD

St. Domingo Road is famous in Liverpool because of its Sunday school being the origins of what became Everton Football club who once played at nearby Anfield. The southern most, top end of this road is one of the highest points in Liverpool, on Everton ridge and therefore was where the Beacon was situated from about the 13th century, giving rise to the nearby Beacon Lane. That site is now occupied by the innovative Iron Church of St. George, designed and built by Thomas Rickman and John Cragg in 1814. The exterior is of traditional stone, the interior of pre-cast iron, bolted together on site. There is now a viewpoint which overlooks the city to the west, across the Mersey to Wirral and to the Welsh mountains beyond.

The name St. Domingo itself is named in commemoration of a prize captured in San Domingo by wealthy West India merchant and sugar refiner, George Campbell. Campbell sailed a privateer and from his haul built an estate and Mansion House calling it St. Domingo House. He became Lord Mayor of Liverpool in 1763 and has a street named after him off Duke Street. Mere Lane which runs off St. Domingo Road to the east, led to a small lake known as St. Domingo Pit which when frozen during the winter provided a skating rink for the locals. The site now is the junction with Robson Street and Breckfield Road North.

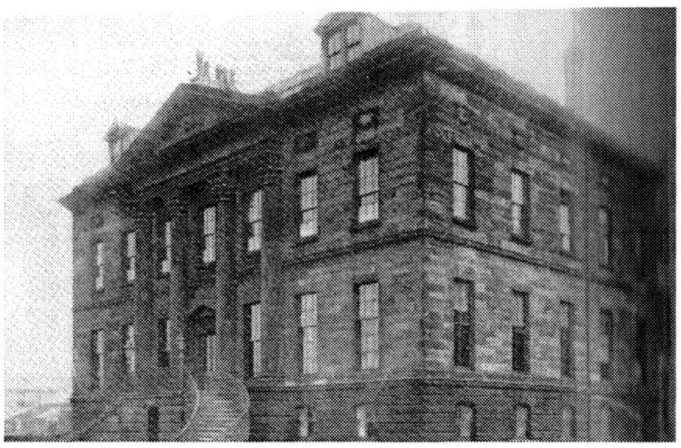

Grandiose St. Domingo House, demolished for a tenement complex. Almost seems criminal doesn't it?

After changing ownership and being rebuilt over the years, St. Domingo House, as elegant as it was with its sweeping staircase entrance was demolished in the mid 1930s, the land being used for the construction of Sir Thomas White Gardens tenement development. These were named after a former leader of the city's Conservative party and J.P. White began life as a cabin boy, returning to Liverpool to become a licensed victualler. In 1919 he entered politics under the guidance of Sir Archibald Salvidge, becoming chairman of four committees, namely the tramways and Electricity, the Housing, the joint Mersey Tunnel and the Speke Airport Development Committee.

The five storey blocks were built south of the Liverpool Corporation yard around Penrose Street, part of the original sandstone wall of St. Domingo House being used as the perimeter wall. They were situated immediately behind Pugin's Church of Our Lady Immaculate. This, in 1856 was built as the Lady and Chancel Chapel of the first proposed Roman Catholic Cathedral which was discontinued as the money required was deemed more necessary for local schools. The flats were demolished in 1984.

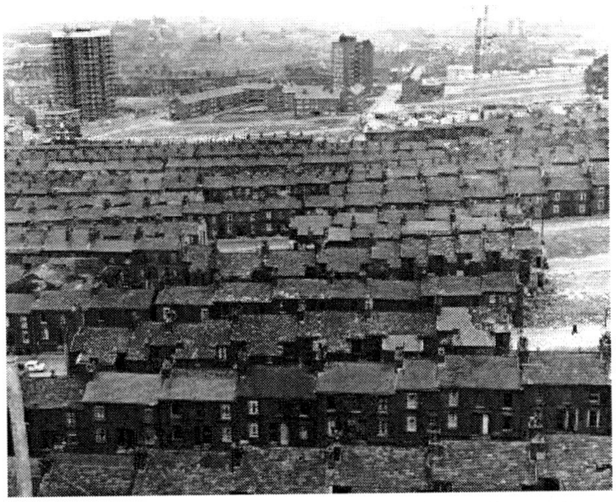

A 1965 view from the top of Millburn Heights on Conway Street. Marwood and Medea Towers can be seen whilst cranes start work on Candia and Crete Towers.

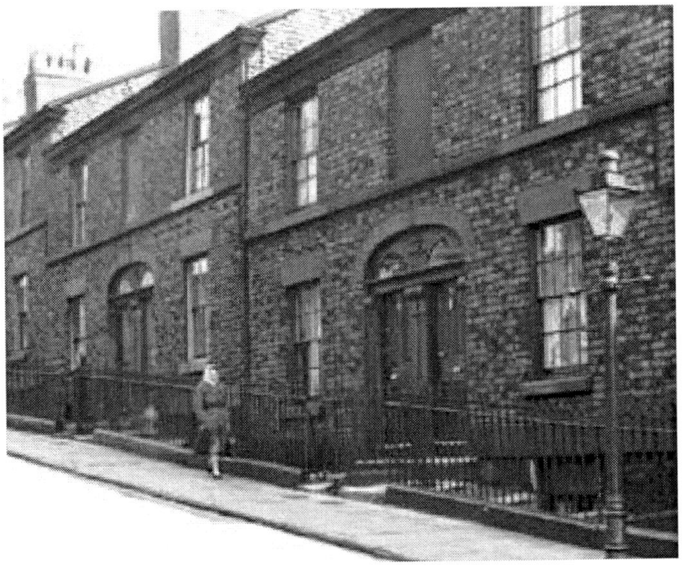

Conway Street in 1958. Many of the streets leading up to Everton ridge were very steep, much to the delight of local children when it snowed.

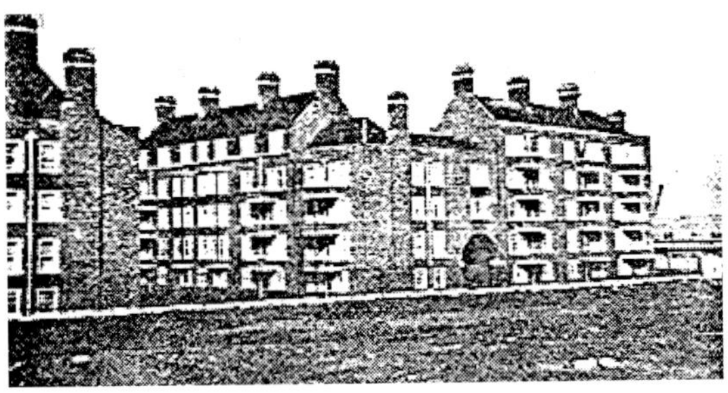

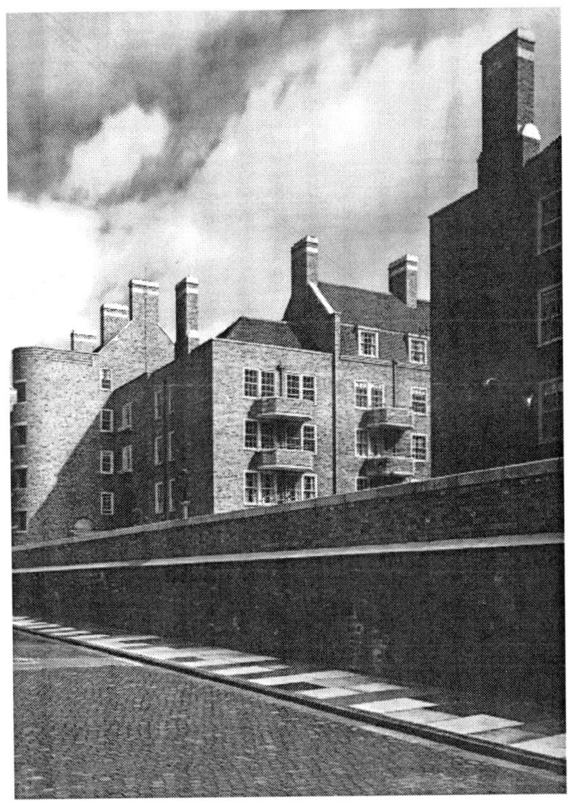

A 1938 view of part of the new tenements incorporating the original sandstone wall from St. Domnigo House and another view in the 1970s.

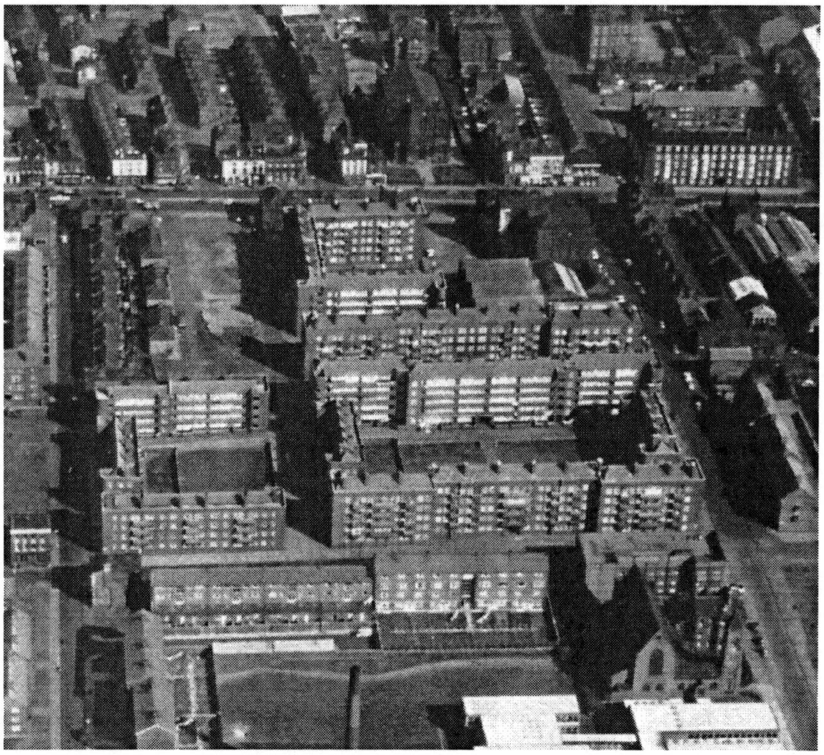

An aerial view of Woodstock, Ashfield and Hopwood Gardens with Wilbraham House visible across Scotland Road

SCOTLAND ROAD

To the south of Boundary Street which once marked the ancient boundary between Liverpool and Kirkdale, a huge slum clearance programme was undertaken in the early 1930s. Westmoreland Place, Woodstock Street and the north end of Limekiln Lane were cleared in 1933 to allow for the building of three tenement complexes.

Hopwood Gardens, at four storeys, fronted onto Hopwood Street, whilst Ashfield Gardens at five storeys fronted onto Westmoreland place facing Benledi Street area housing office. The larger development of Woodstock Gardens which was also five storeys was bounded by Latimer Street, Silvester Street and Limekiln Lane. As a whole, they formed a large community servicing the parishes of St. Silvester's and St. Anthony's.

A lot of the residents from here found local employment in industries 'over the bridge' on Athol Street and alongside the Leeds/Liverpool canal. Other major employers in the area were the British American Tobacco factory and Tillotsons packaging on Commercial Road. These dwellings succumbed to their own clearance programme in 1983.

A slightly smaller development of tenement flats stood across Scotland Road between Penrhyn Street and Wilbraham Street named Wilbraham House. A local pastime for many residents living here was the 'Derby' cinema, situated on the corner of Wilbraham Street which has been a funeral parlour for some years now. A petrol station and new housing now stand on the site of the blocks.

Further down Scotland Road heading towards the City Centre stood a block of tenements whose demise was brought about as they stood directly in the path of the Kingway Mersey Tunnel approach roads. Built in 1931, Lawrence Gardens, a C' shaped block of flats had landings which faced out along its length towards Lawrence Street and also towards Cazneau Street to the east and onto Scotland Road in the west. This created a 'backie' which faced south.

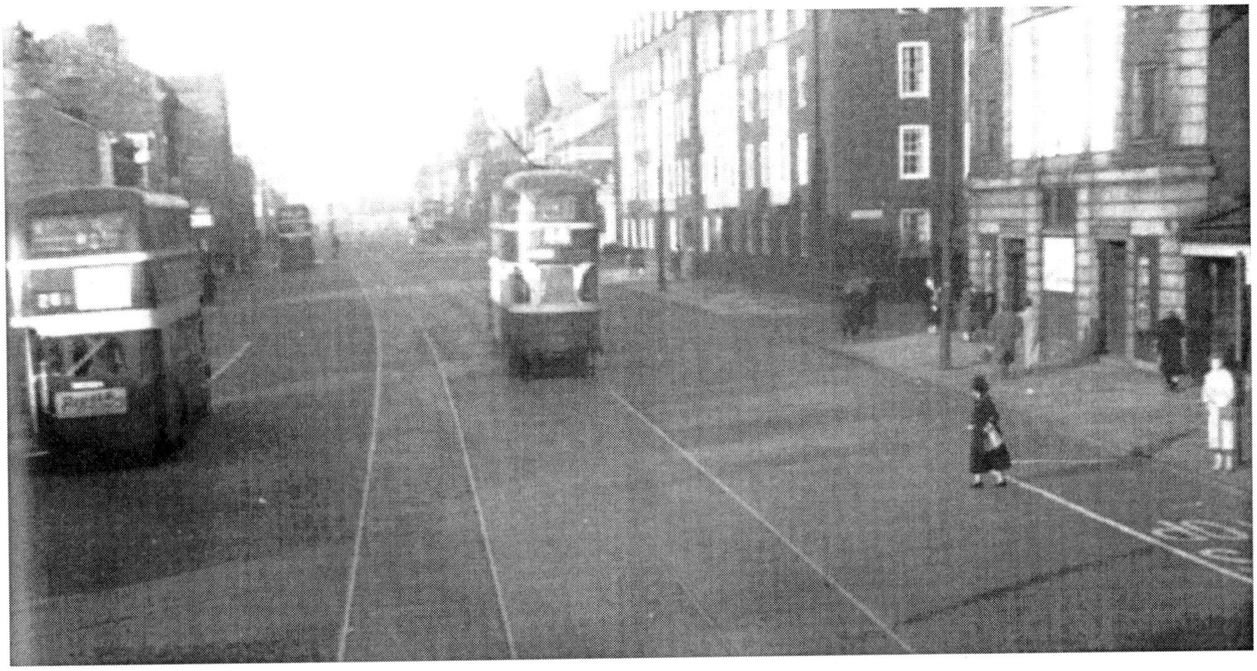

Autumn 1956 and the 44 is the only tram route serving the north end of Scotland Road just one year before the last ever Liverpool tram. Wilbraham House tenements and the Derby Picturehouse (1912-1960) which began life as a United Methodist Free Church are visible on the right. The 28 open back bus proceeds past the top of St. Martins Street en route to Netherton.

As in most cases with these blocks, not a great deal of thought was given in keeping the grassed and weed rampant areas clear for enjoyment and they fell into decay during the 1970s and were demolished. Many residents were upset at having to leave this area for the sake of a roadway which decimated the once proud Scotland Road. The site was next occupied by Whitbreads brewery who had relocated from cramped premises in Trueman Street off Dale Street. Their stay was short lived and the premises were converted into a wholesale warehouse by Bestway.

The southern most block of tenements on Scottie had long since gone before the new road scheme took hold. Chaucer House on the corner of Juvenal Street contained 120 flats which fronted onto Nash Grove. It is one of the few blocks that were demolished only for its site to lay barren as wasteland for many years. Still to this day, the east side of Scotland Road in this area is taken up by a grass verge.

The purpose of this Liverpool City Engineer's photograph was to record 172 Scotland Road. In this scene from 1949, the backdrop is of Victoria Square Dwellings.

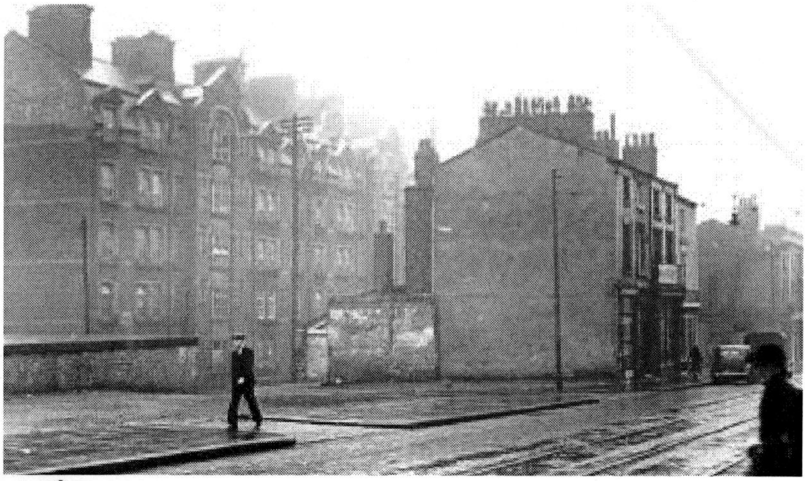

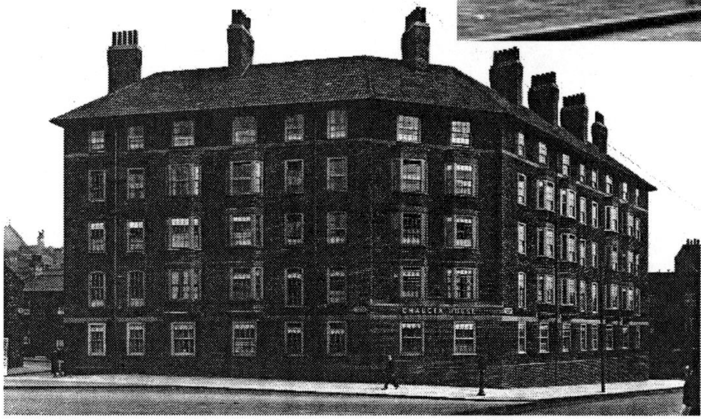

Chaucer House on the corner of Scotland Road and Juvenal Street with Nash Grove in the background. This block had come and gone by the time I was hanging around this area

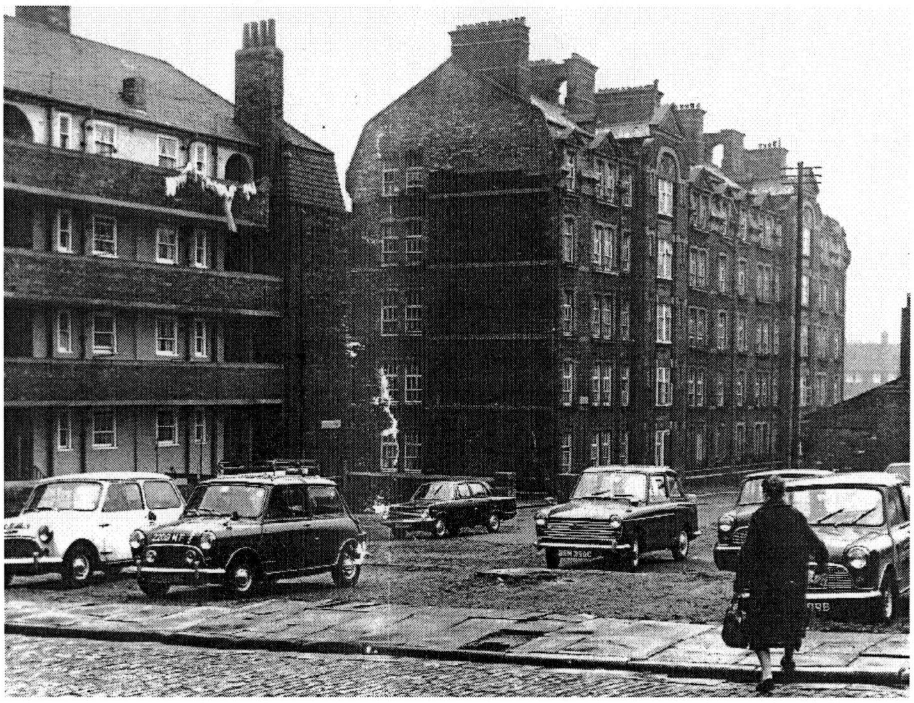

A 1966 shot of McKee Street viewed from Lawrence Street (both now abolished). Lawrence Gardens is on the left standing beside Victoria Square which was demolished later the same year. This whole area lay barren throughout the 1970s, isolated as an island by the Kingsway tunnel approach roads.

VAUXHALL ROAD

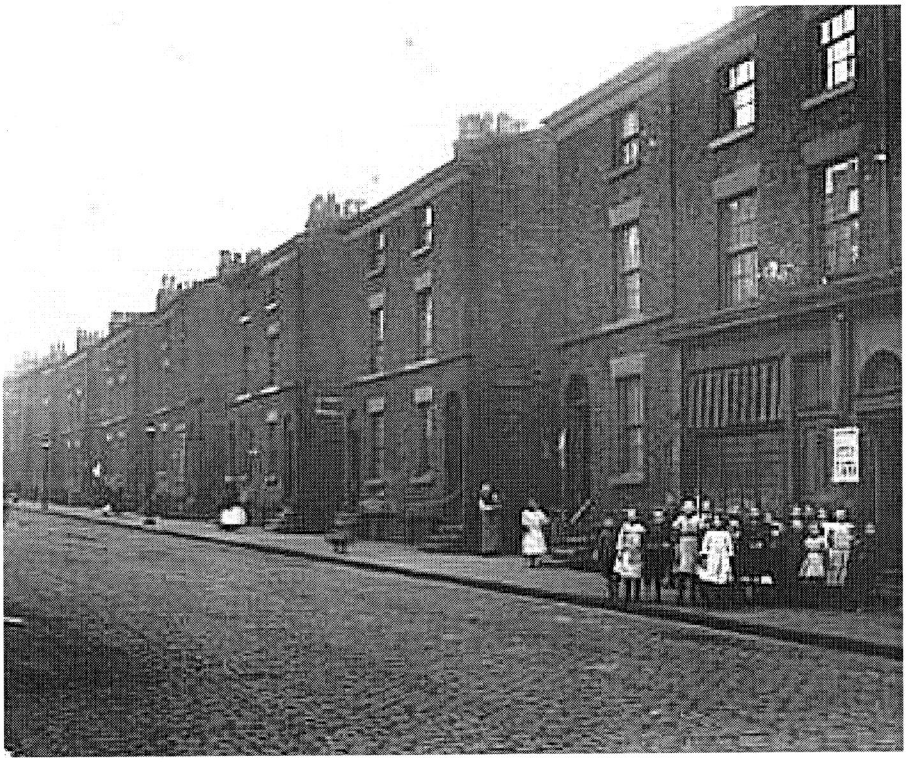

Due west from Lawrence Gardens, on the opposite side of Scotland Road runs Burlington Street in a gradient down to and beyond Vauxhall Road. At its junction with Pall Mall stood one of the areas biggest employers, the Tate & Lyle sugar refinery which employed around 3000 people, many of them local. On the city side of Burlington Street stood tenements built in 1925 to replace dilapidated terracing and courts from a hundred years earlier.

Looking up Burlington Street 1920. Tenements were to replace these by the end of the decade

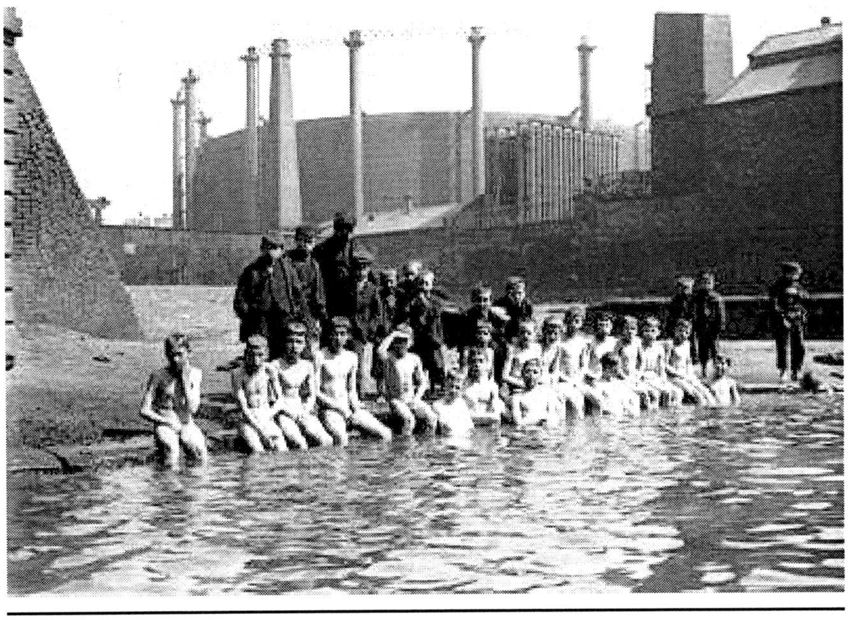

Known as the water rats, local boys take to the Tates warmed Leeds/Liverpool canal by the Burlington Street bridge.

The old and the new. Portland Gardens and the new housing

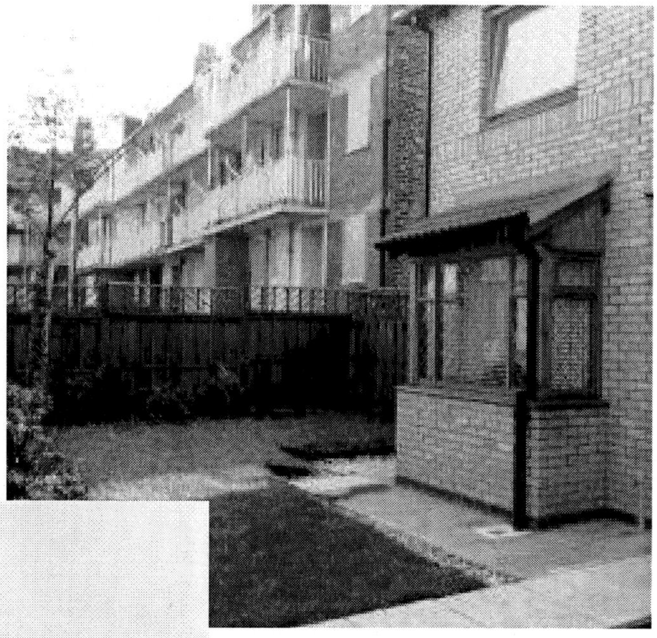

The new tenements take pride of place on the south side of Burlington Street.

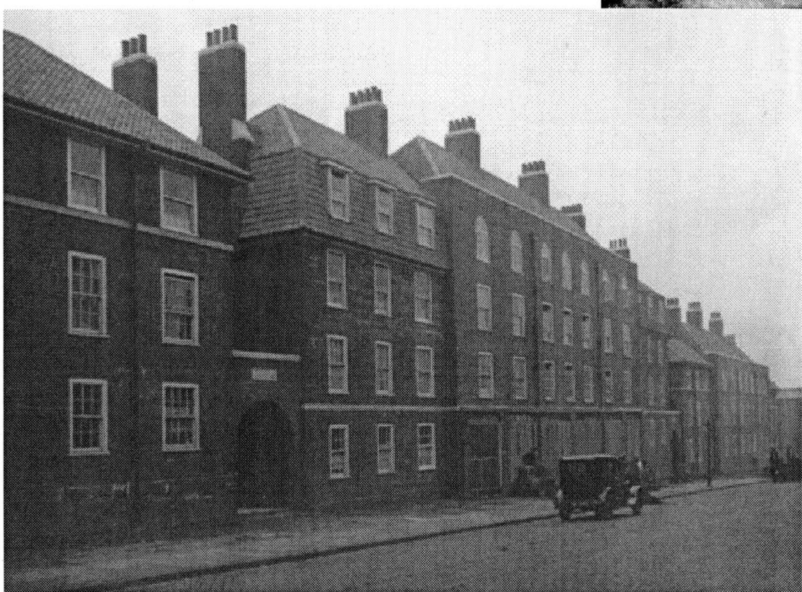

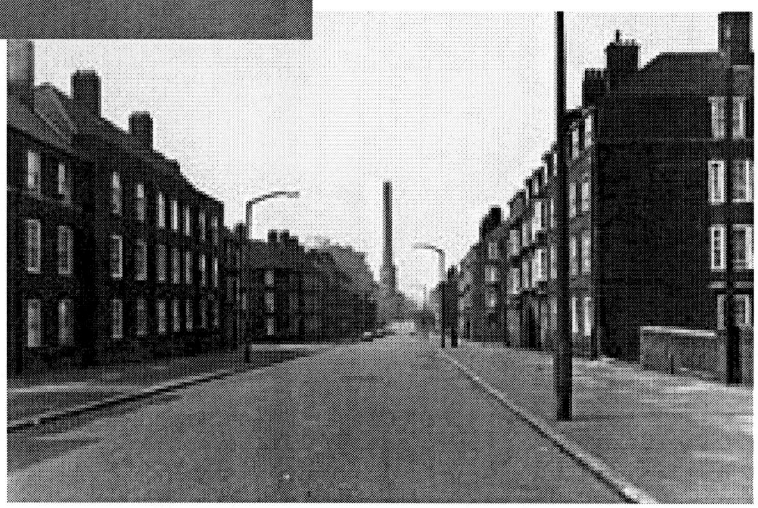

Looking west down Burlington Street towards Tate & Lyles Sugar Refinery.

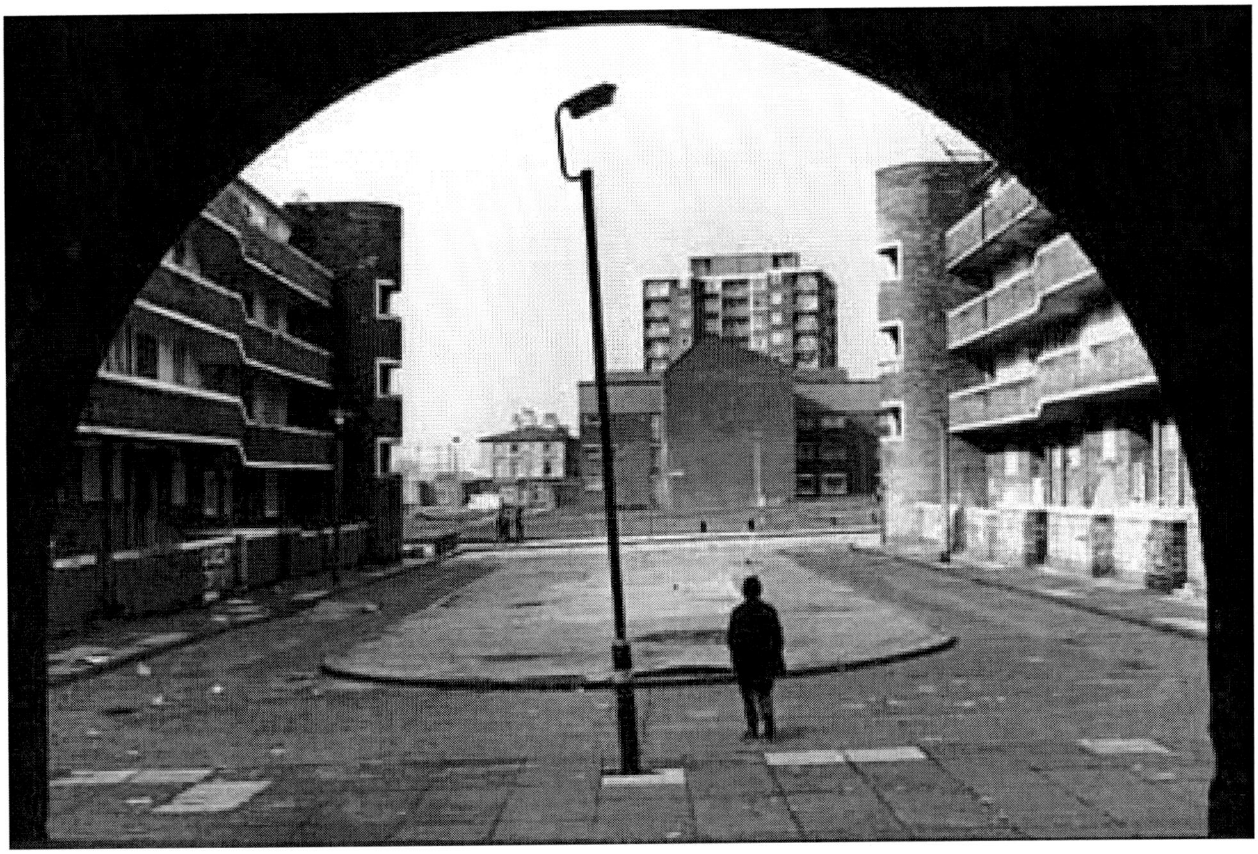

Portland Gardens looking north across Green Street towards James Clarke Street and the Castle Public House and Tatlock Towers on Tatlock Street.

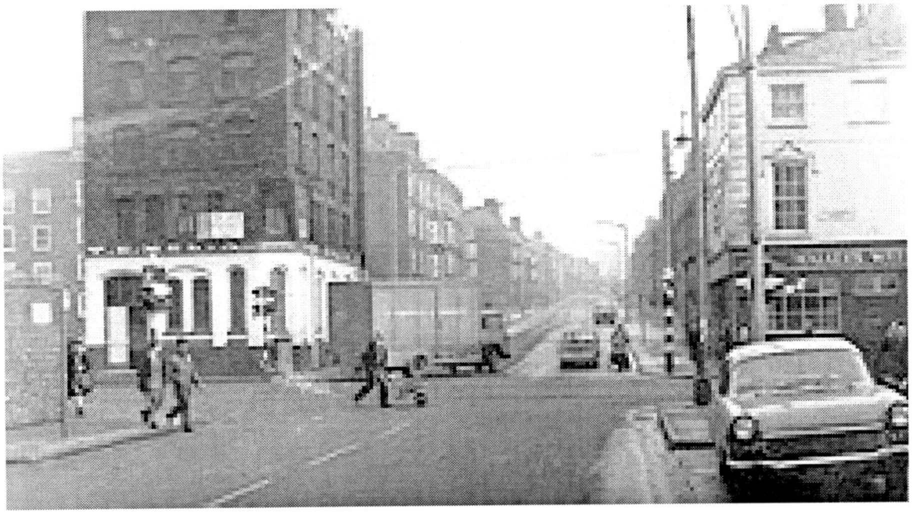

Looking up Burlington Street across its junction with Vauxhall Road

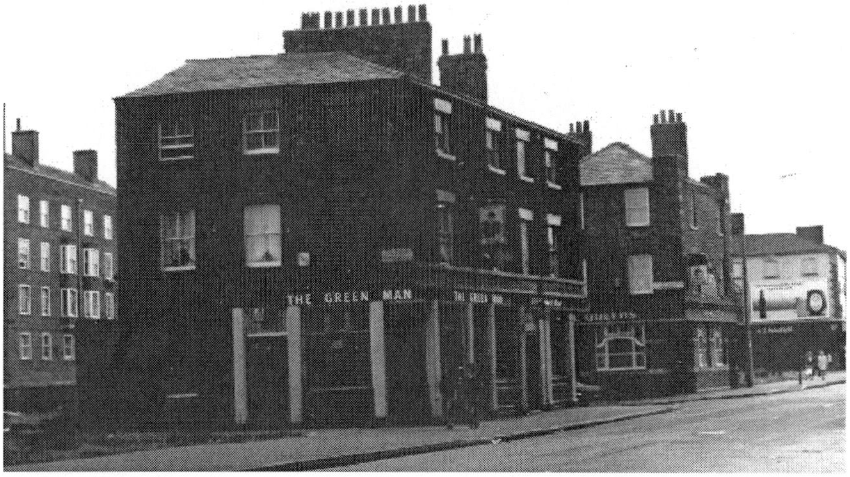

Vauxhall Road. The Queens has gone but the Green Man from 'Boys from the black stuff' fame is still going strong. Portland Gardens can be seen behind.

Eldon Street housed similar style blocks whose landings faced across garages on Bond Street to their neighbours on Burlington Street. On the north side of 'Burly' stood Portland Gardens, built a decade later. These fronted across Portland Street which ran up to Mile End and formed two large squares either side of Titchfield Street. In 1989 a majority of these blocks were demolished with the lower blocks to the rear of the Green Man public house being converted to sheltered accommodation for the elderly. The Eldonian Housing Co-operative was born out of the passion of the residents of this area to keep their communities together instead of being shipped out to new towns in the back of beyond like the Scottie Roaders of the 1950s and 60s. With little help from the ruling Labour powers in Liverpool who saw this scheme as elitist, money was sought from Central Government and the award winning Eldonian Village was created on wasteland along the banks of the Liverpool/Leeds canal. On Vauxhall Road, between Blackstock Street and Paul Street stood the tenement blocks of Blackstock Gardens. Completed in 1934, they incorporated a corner shop, originally called Pegrams. They replaced a row of slum and derelict commercial properties including the No.7 branch of the TGWU and Lever Brothers transport depot. Tragedy befell the local community of these blocks and the commuters of two packed trams when on 20th December 1940, whilst taking refuge in the central air raid shelter, German bombers scored a direct hit killing up to 200 poor souls. News censorship during the war kept this

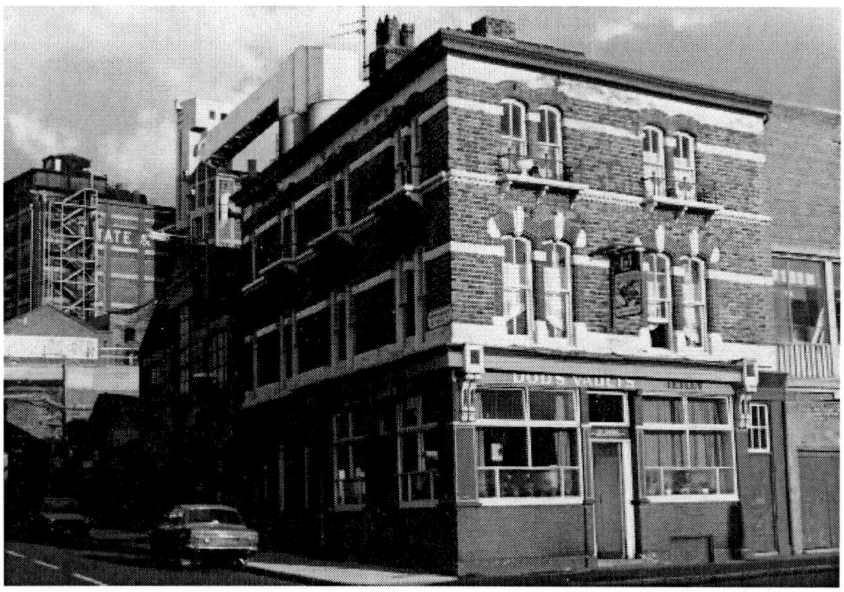

Dods Vaults on the corner of Great Howard Street and Sprainger Street is separated from the Tate & Lyle complex by the Exchange Station railway line.

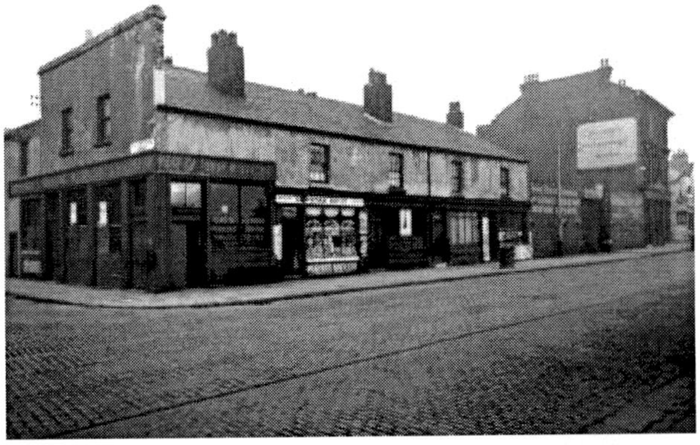

Vauxhall Road between Blackstock Street and Paul Street in 1932. The area would be transformed within a couple of years. Here, are shown buildings due for demolition including a branch of the TGWU, a tobacconists and a Lever Bros SPD Transport Depot.

low key but there now stands a memorial to those who lost their lives facing the old site of the tenements. Between Leeds Street and Tithebarn Street to the west of Vauxhall Road stood Vauxhall Gardens and Highfield Gardens. A number of slum dwellings and commercial properties on Northampton Street, Upper Milk Street, Worfield Street, Union Place and Tomlin Street were cleared in 1933. These included the Smithy brewery, cloth stores and produce depots that were prevalent in the vicinity. One such premises did survive though which became known locally as the 'spuddie' and which stood between one part of Vauxhall Gardens and another block on Westmoreland Street. This community was served largely by St. Mary's Highfield parish until the tenements were demolished in the early 1990s. The church, itself a replacement for the original that was bombed during WWII, was demolished in 2003 as its congregation suffered. Vauxhall Road, originally Pinfold Lane was once nicknamed 'Spice Island' because of the smells omitted from nearby chemical factories. The road was synonymous with industry such as bone grinding, distilleries, saw mills, tanneries, bonded warehouses, rice and flour mills, sugar refineries, bottling stores, ink works, sack makers, Corporation depots, transport premises and coal yards due to its close proximity with the dock system and the Liverpool/Leeds canal.

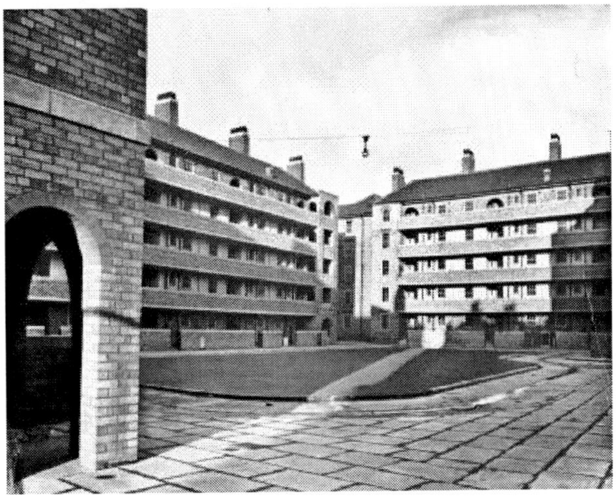

Blackstock Gardens newly completed in 1934 with a diagonal view across the square where 6 years later, the ill fated air raid shelter was to stand. Another view is from Blackstock Street itself.

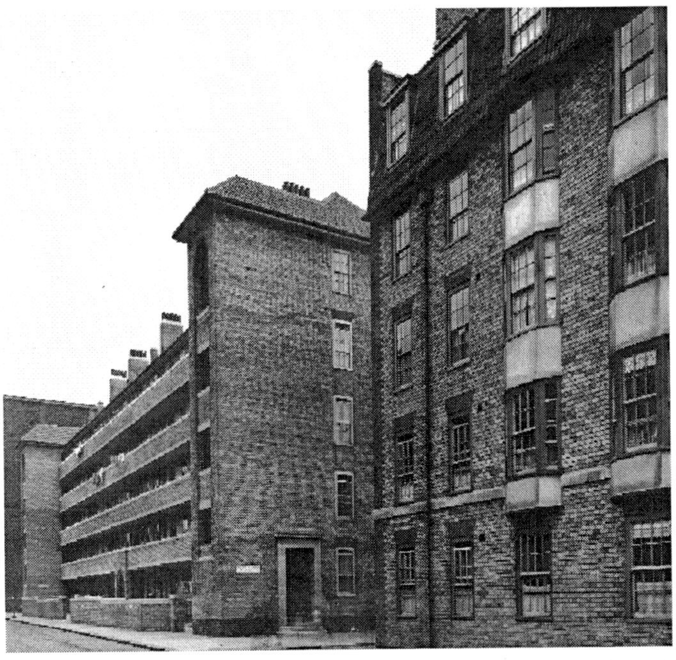

Tithebarn Street looking West towards the Pier Head. A flock of sheep are being hand driven up the street towards market in this 1915 view.

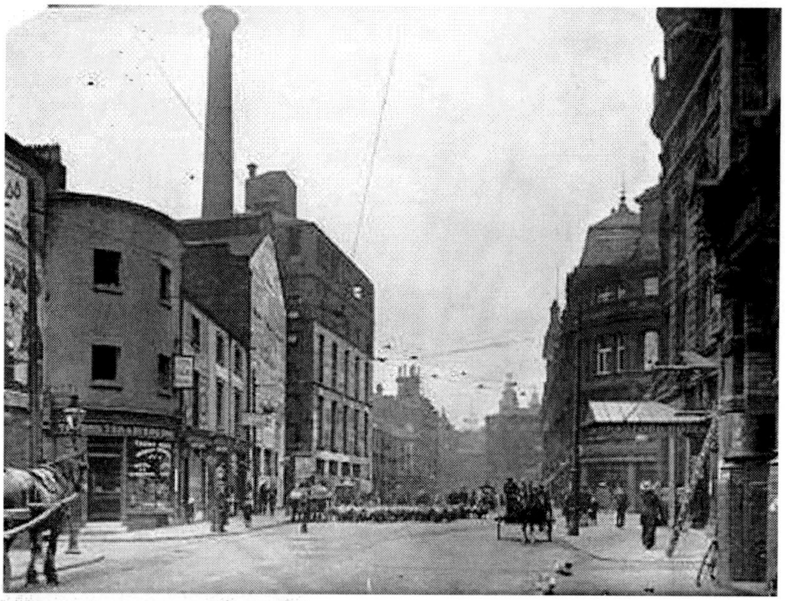

Looking East down Great Crosshall Street in 1966. The End block in the middle of the picture was sacrificed for the Eastbound Churchill Way flyover a couple of years later so never saw its 18th birthday. Bispham House is being built to the left and Fontenoy Gardens and Cartwright House tenements are in view..

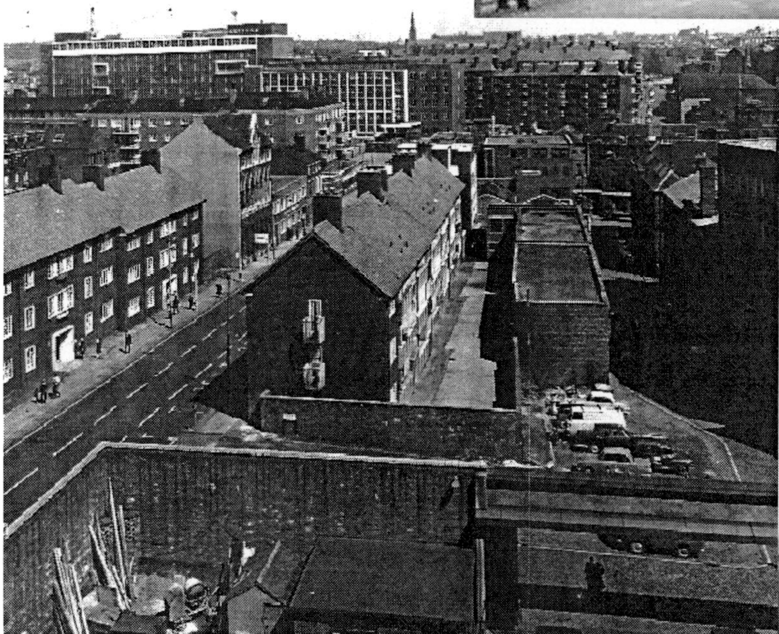

One of Liverpool's earliest electricity supplies came from the Pumpfields generating station off Vauxhall Road. Vauxhall itself was the name of a house that once stood on the banks of the previously mentioned canal.

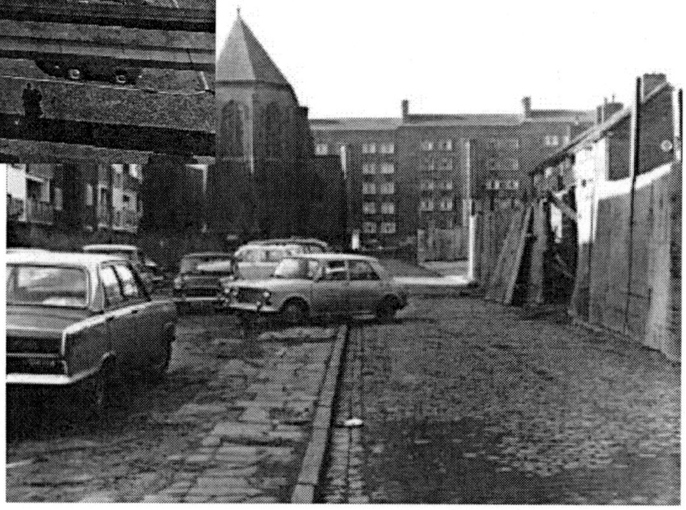

Looking West up Lace Street towards Holy Cross Church and Standish Street flats. In this January 1967 photograph, Bispham House is being constructed on the right of the street behind the tins that are visible.

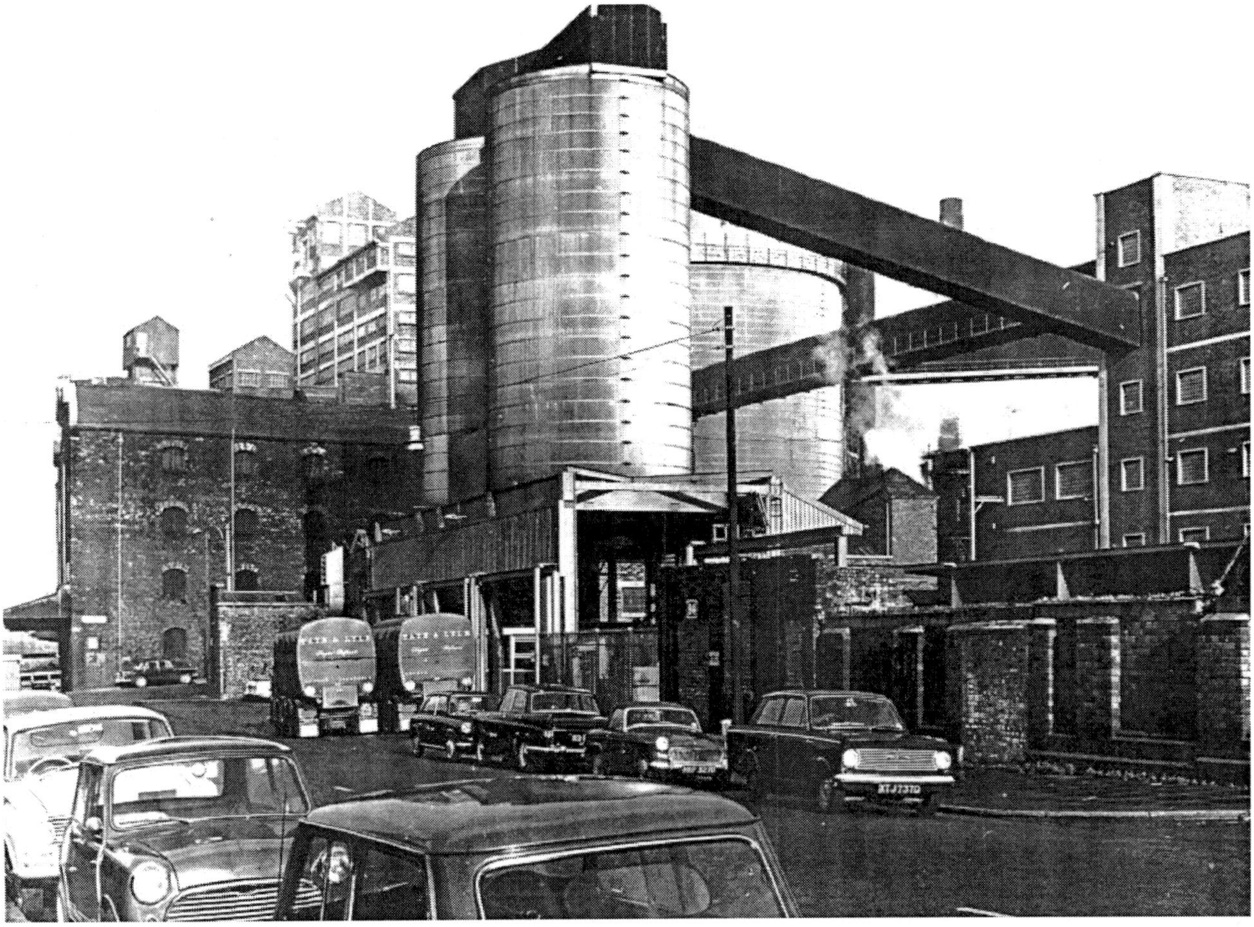

Tate & Lyle Sugar Refinery is at full blast here in 1967. This is Pall Mall with Chisenhale Street in the background. A 60s view of a prestige car lot.

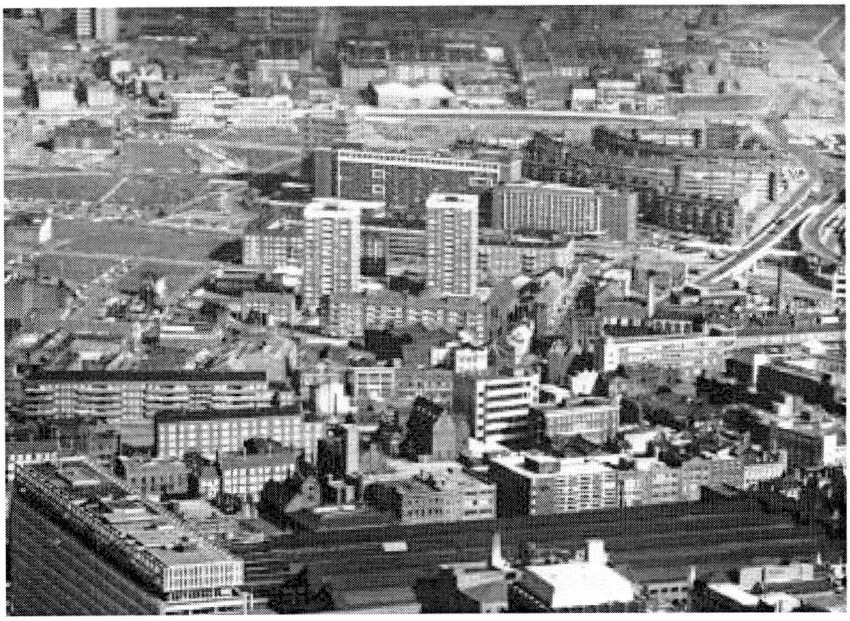

Beyond the Littlewoods building are Highfield and Vauxhall Gardens. Adlington and Bispham House stand over Fontenoy Gardens and beyond the John Moores University are Gerard Crescent and Gerard Gardens. Great Richmond Street's block and the four squares can be seen in the background

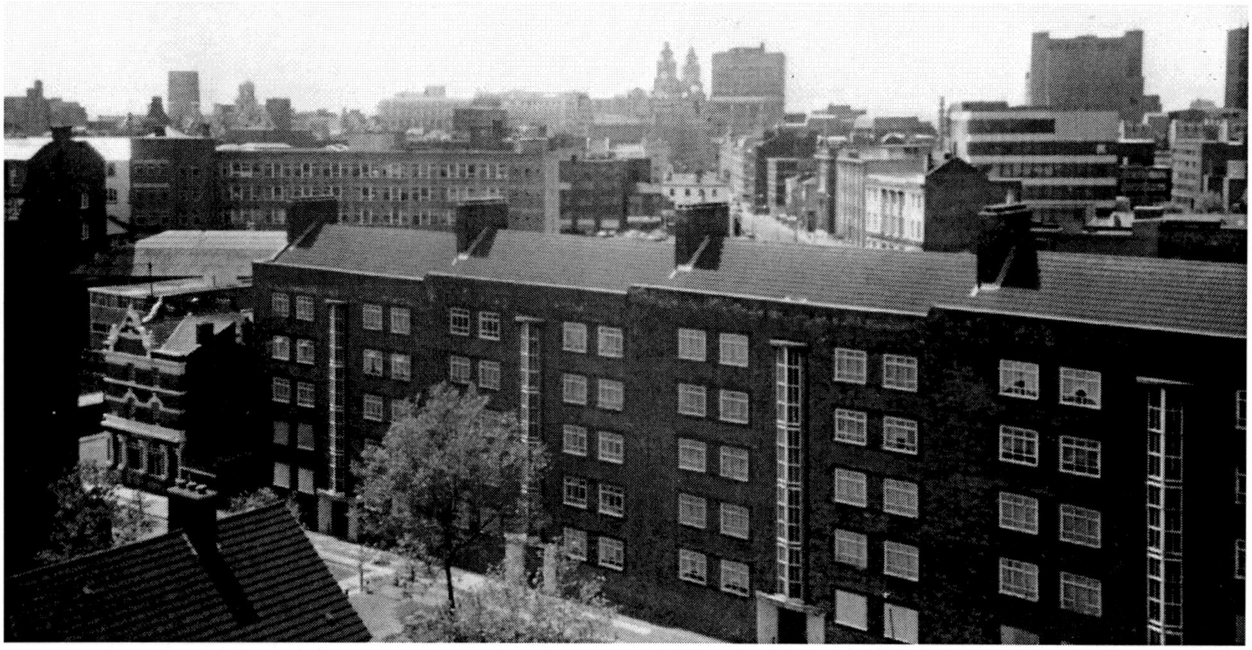

Standish Street 'Coffin' blocks, so called because of their diagonally tapered gable end can be seen here off Great Crosshall Street. The Borough Public House, once owned by Riverside Labour MP Bob Parry still stands today.

Highfield Gardens on Highfield Street made way for new flats whilst the Rose & Crown Public House known locally as Bragier's was refurbished and integrated into the new development and renamed 'Time Out'.

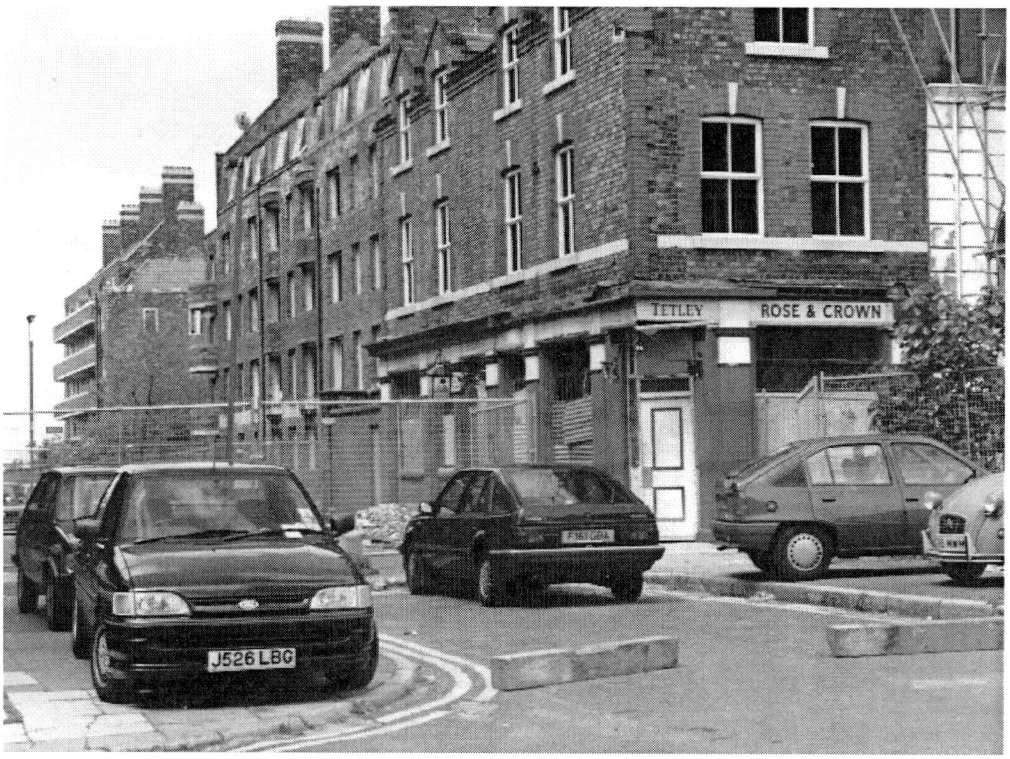

Vauxhall Gardens in 1990. Old and tired but only run down because of Council policy at the time.

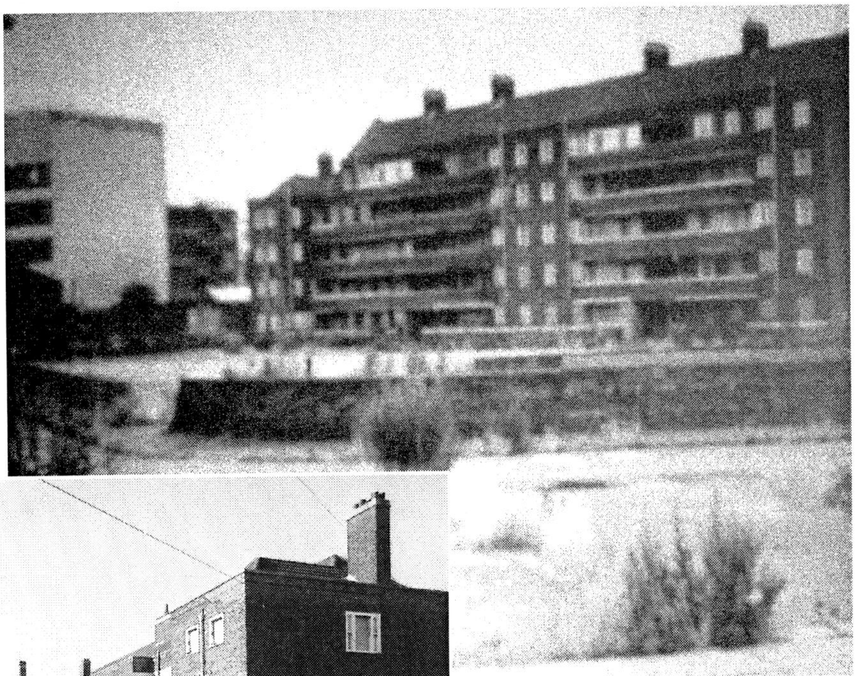

Part of Vauxhall Gardens off Leeds Street, looking towards the block on Westmoreland Street and others behind on Upper Milk Street. The Littlewoods Building on Old Hall Street can be seen as can the dilapidation of the area.

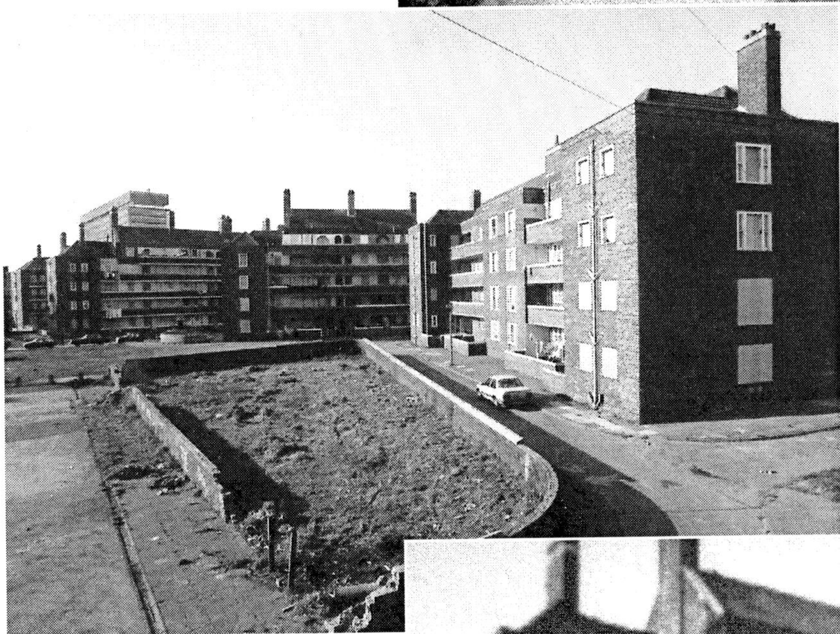

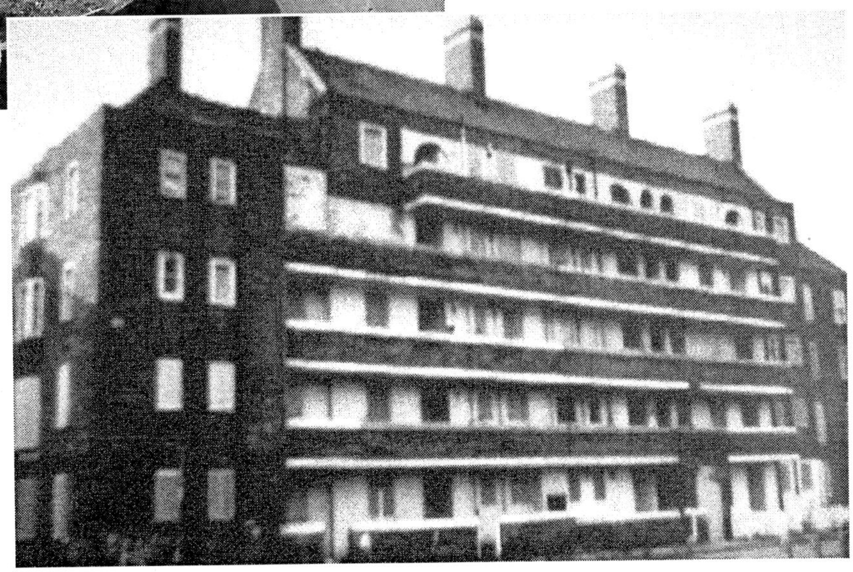

Upper Milk Street flats. Part of the Vauxy and Highfy development.

BYROM STREET

Construction of Fontenoy Gardens was commenced in 1935, the first part being the L shaped section that took the Fontenoy Street/Addison Street corner on the site of Duckworth Street Saw Mill. This was the only part of 'Fonney Oy', as it was known locally, to contain ground floor flats. Old property was then demolished on Byrom Street and Hodson Street to allow for the continuation of the tenements, the join hardly noticeable.

This larger section housed a row of shops at ground floor level beneath a canopy. Part of this housed the Holy Cross school dinner hall as well as the Vauxhall Neighbourhood Council headquarters in the 1970s. In 1940, the first 'British Restaurant' was located here, pioneered by Liverpool Corporation, these offered affordable meals during wartime Liverpool with the emphasis being on saving power and electricity in the home.

A second section of the development was constructed on the south side of the Waterloo dock railway cutting which separated these flats, these backed onto Great Crosshall Street. The Central careers and housing offices were situated on the ground floor of this block during the 1970s, the whole complex having been completed by 1940.

The building of the 2nd Mersey road tunnel, Kingsway, had resulted in the demise of the area immediately north of these blocks. Commencing around 1966, Addison Street, right up past Mile End and Bevington Bush was decimated resulting in the local communities becoming involved in a documentary made in 1969 entitled 'Us and Them.' Them being the council riding roughshod over the good people of Scotland Road in favour of a Mersey crossing that would have been more suited geographically towards the south end of the city since the existing Queensway tunnel was already only a mile down the road.

Fearing objections and delays from the middle classes in the leafy suburbs of Aigburth, it stood to reason that there would be less

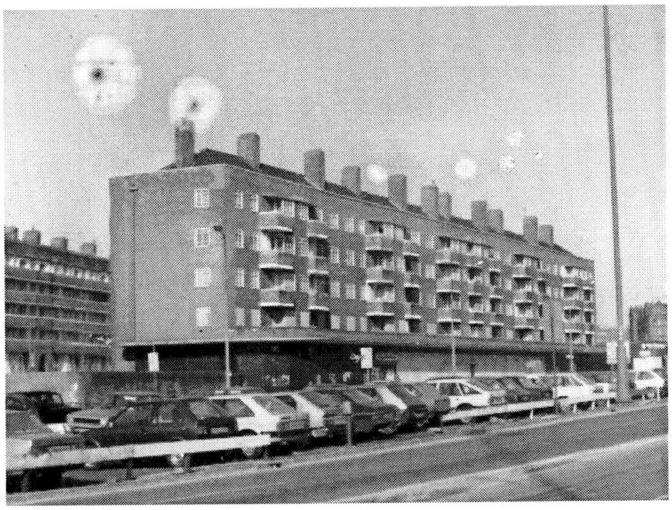

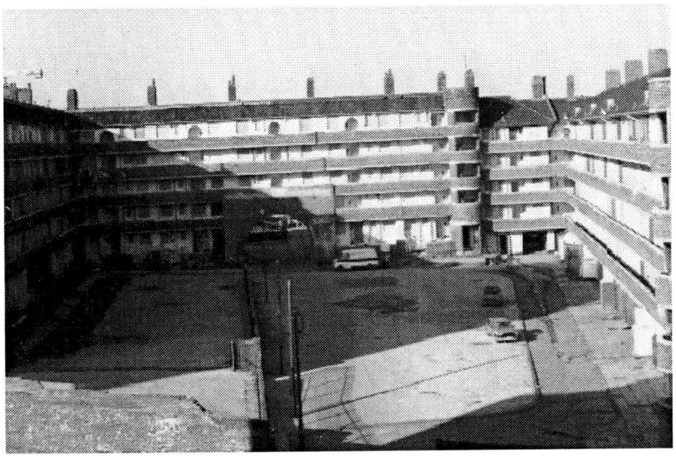

opposition from the council tenants of inner city tenements. There wasn't, but that didn't seem to matter. That documentary and another against the proposed ring road from 1978 entitled 'Homes not Roads', narrated by Brian Jacques argued that the pedestrian walkovers placed across the now more busy Byrom Street were more like obstacle courses and that the area was now fragmented into smaller ghettos, each too small to warrant their own vital amenities like a post office, chemist or doctors surgery.

Fonney Oy was demolished in 1987 with only a few dozen houses and bungalows now occupying the same area of space. Byrom street had now seen many changes since its origins as Towns End Lane when it was once the boundary at the top of Dale Street. As the town grew, it was renamed Dog Kennel Lane because of the neighbouring kennels belonging to the Corporations pack of hounds. The current name derives from a local building contractor, George Byrom who had a yard nearby.

Fontenoy Gardens Byrom Street block with ground level shops and Arden House in the background. Another shot shows the square looking a bit worse for wear shortly before demolition.

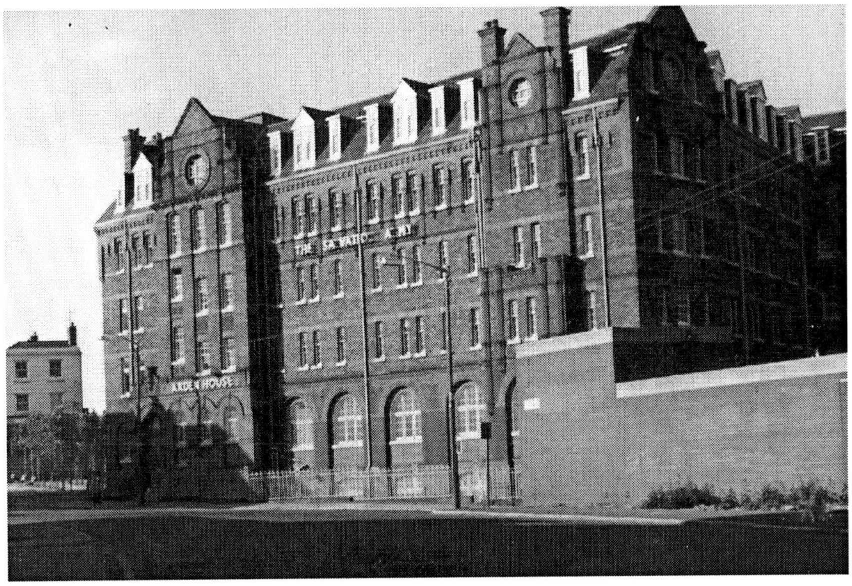

Arden House Salvation Army Hostel on Bevington Bush and the Wellington Public House now both consigned to history.

HUNTER STREET/ CHRISTIAN STREET

Across Byrom Street, up until the mid 1930s were some of the most dilapidated slum terracing in the city centre. It was this area that had earlier led Dr. William Henry Duncan to declare as the most unsanitary in the city. Hunter Street, Gerard Street and Circus Street were Liverpool's 'Little Italy' and these were the three principal streets which led up to Christian Street with a myriad of courts and terraces in between. The top end of these streets were the first to be demolished to allow for the construction of Gerard Gardens. The foundation stone was laid on 21st June 1935 by the Right Honourable Sir Kingsley Wood MP who was the minister for health on the same day as that for St. Andrews Gardens on Copperas Hill.

Residents were already inhabiting this baseball stadium shaped arena as construction of neighbouring Gerard Crescent went on behind it. A documentary film was made in 1938 by Liverpool Corporation in conjunction with Liverpool Gas Co. called 'Homes for Workers' detailing Housing minister, Lancelot Keay's vision for the future. Central to this was rare motion footage of the on-going construction of Gerard Crescent and its facing blocks, there being only three at the time, Cartwright, Lionel and Downe House, Thurlow being constructed a year later.

Containing almost 400 flats once completed, the area was revamped with Hunter Street and Christian Street becoming main roads for traffic transiting from Scotland Road to Islington and from Lime Street to Scotland Road respectively. With the addition of the Churchill Way flyovers at the end of the 1960s and the reconstruction of New Islington, the roads surrounding Gerard Gardens were becoming main thoroughfares with no less than twenty established bus routes passing or stopping outside the tenements.

More a stroke of luck then that couldn't have been foreseen, that Lancelot Keay chose these blocks to house two pieces of sculpture he had commissioned from Herbert Tyson Smith. One was of an architect, in Keay's likeness complete with plans of Gerard Gardens,

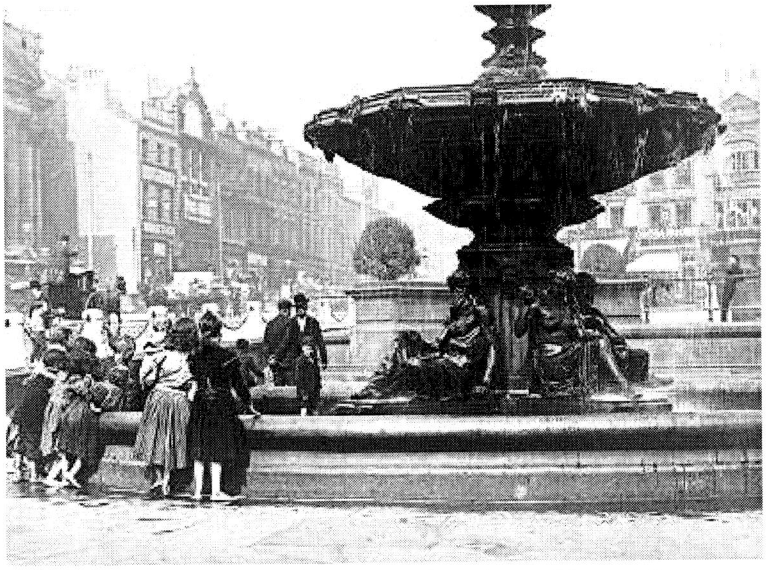

Summer 1901. Street urchins play at the Steble Fountain some 70 years before the street urchin who wrote this book would. A horse drawn carriage is proceeding up Islington.

the other a hod carrier, both of which took pride of place for all to see above the two access road entrances to the 'square'.

It was in fact roads that became more important than keeping communities together which were to win the day regarding the demise of these particular blocks. Successive local councils had done little to modernise these tenements save for a gesture in the mid 1970s when a re-roof, gas fires and low level cisterns were installed. The militant Liverpool labour rulers had seen fit to allow the blocks to become run down with no repairs forthcoming, their agenda being a head to head with the Conservative Government leader, Maggie Thatcher. Accusing her of withholding vital funding from the city, Labour went ahead with a new housing scheme boasting 4,800 new homes in the city but borrowing heavily at inflated interest rates to achieve this. Blocks similar to these have been renovated for 21st Century living whilst new apartments are back in vogue as city centre living becomes all the rage again. What price would these have fetched just a few hundred yards from William Brown Street.

They won't catch much sun in all that clobber but it doesn't stop four blokes on a bench in St. John's Gardens in 1928. The backdrop is a soot caked Liverpool Museum..

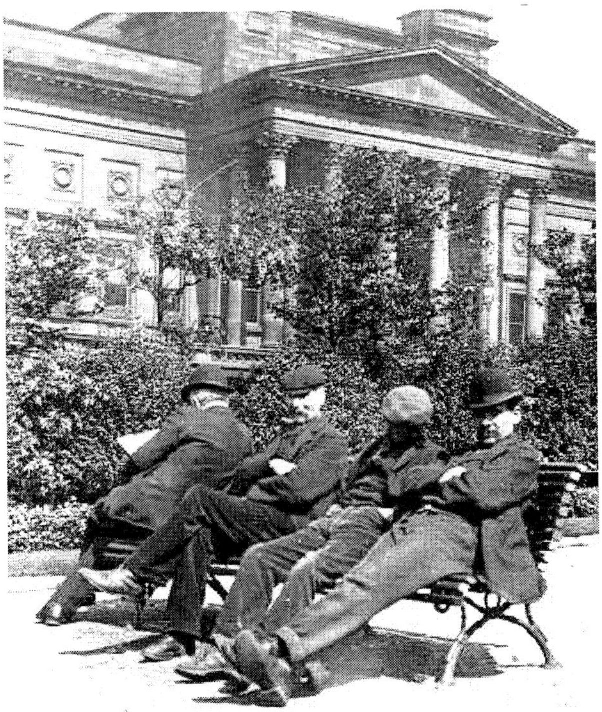

When combined with the westbound and Eastbound flyovers, Hunter Street is now a twelve lane high level and low level inner city motorway for want of a better description. A far cry from its original beginnings as a cobbled street serving the local breweries and friends meeting house, it was named after local tax collector Rowland Hunter who built his home there.

A 1928 view of the Old Haymarket facing the West wall of St. John's Gardens. This property was to be shortly demolished for the Queensway Mersey Tunnel entrance.

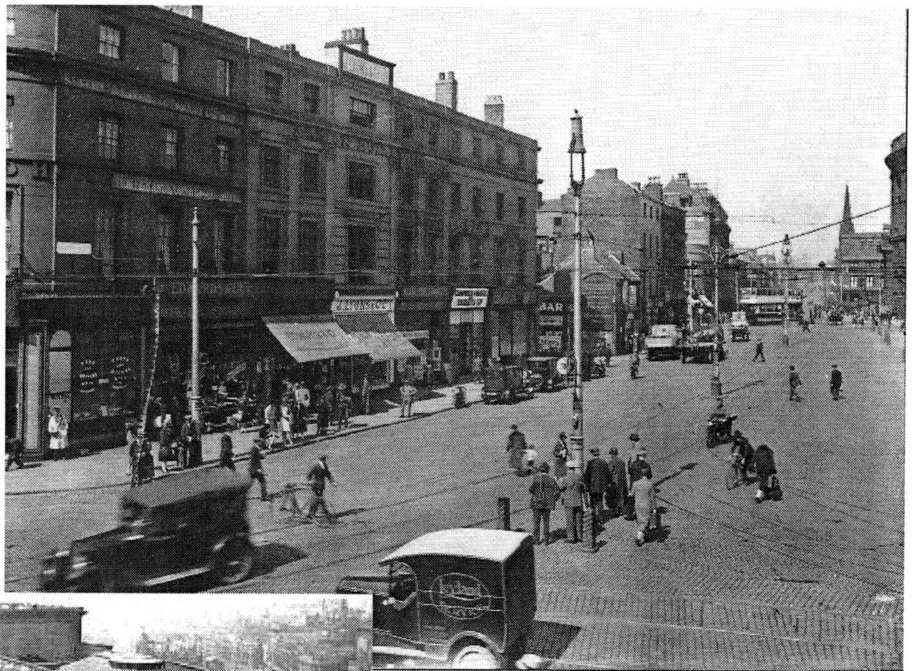

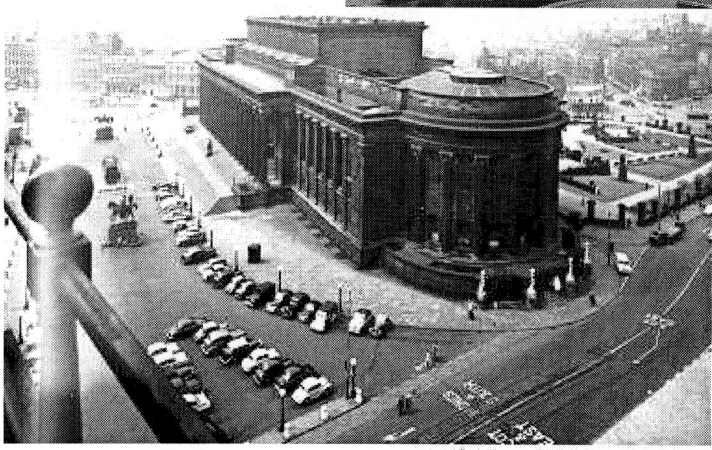

June 1958. St. Georges Hall and Plateau is viewed from the top of the Wellington Column, a stones throw from Gerard Gardens.

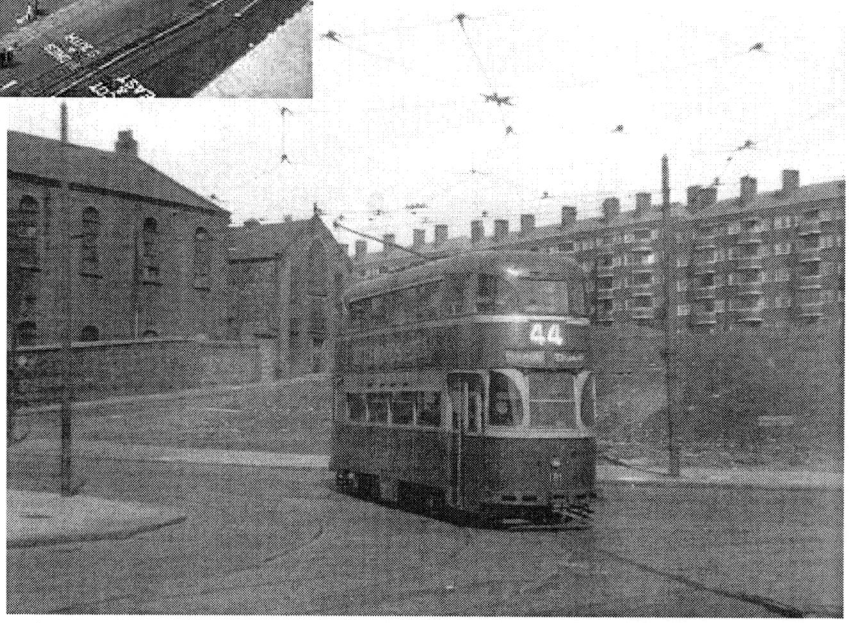

It is Sunday 15th May 1955 and Dale Street is temporarily closed for an Orange Lodge Procession. Bogie Streamliner 181 on the 44 route to the Pier Head therefore has to divert from Byrom Street into Great Crosshall Street where passengers will be shuttled by bus. Downe, Lionel and Cartwright House can be seen in the background. The property from Byrom Terrace to Gerard Street has been demolished but Byrom Hall which takes up the block from Gerard Street to Circus Street still exists. The foreground would become the site for the John Moores University and taken for the widening of Byrom Street.

An aerial view of the Gerard Gardens area in the early 1960s - pre flyovers. The old property on Hunter Street and Cuerdon Street still exists as does the Liverpool Co-operative Society's flagship store, Unity House on Byrom Street. At the top of the picture, Holly Street survives for a few more years and Birkett Street tenements and the Four Squares can be seen along with Holy Trinity Church on St. Anne Street.

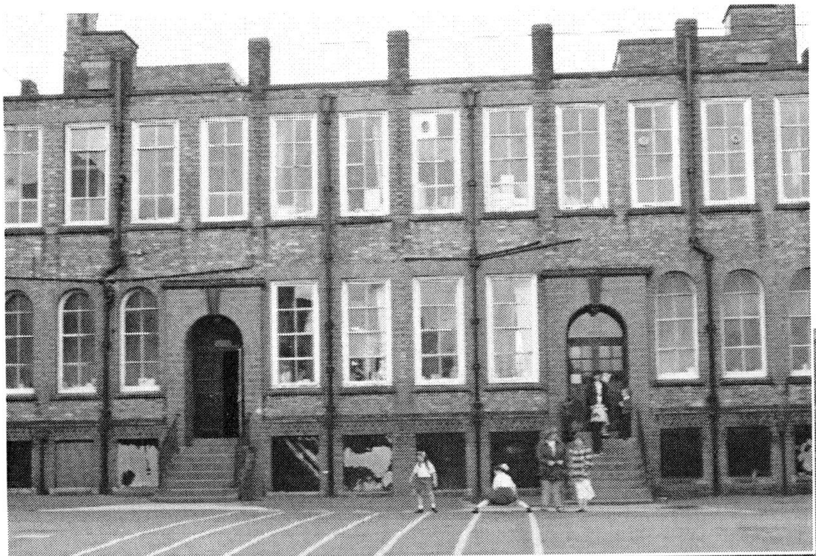

Bishop Goss Junior School on Grosvenor Street also known as St. Joey's. The Educational Institution that produced moi.

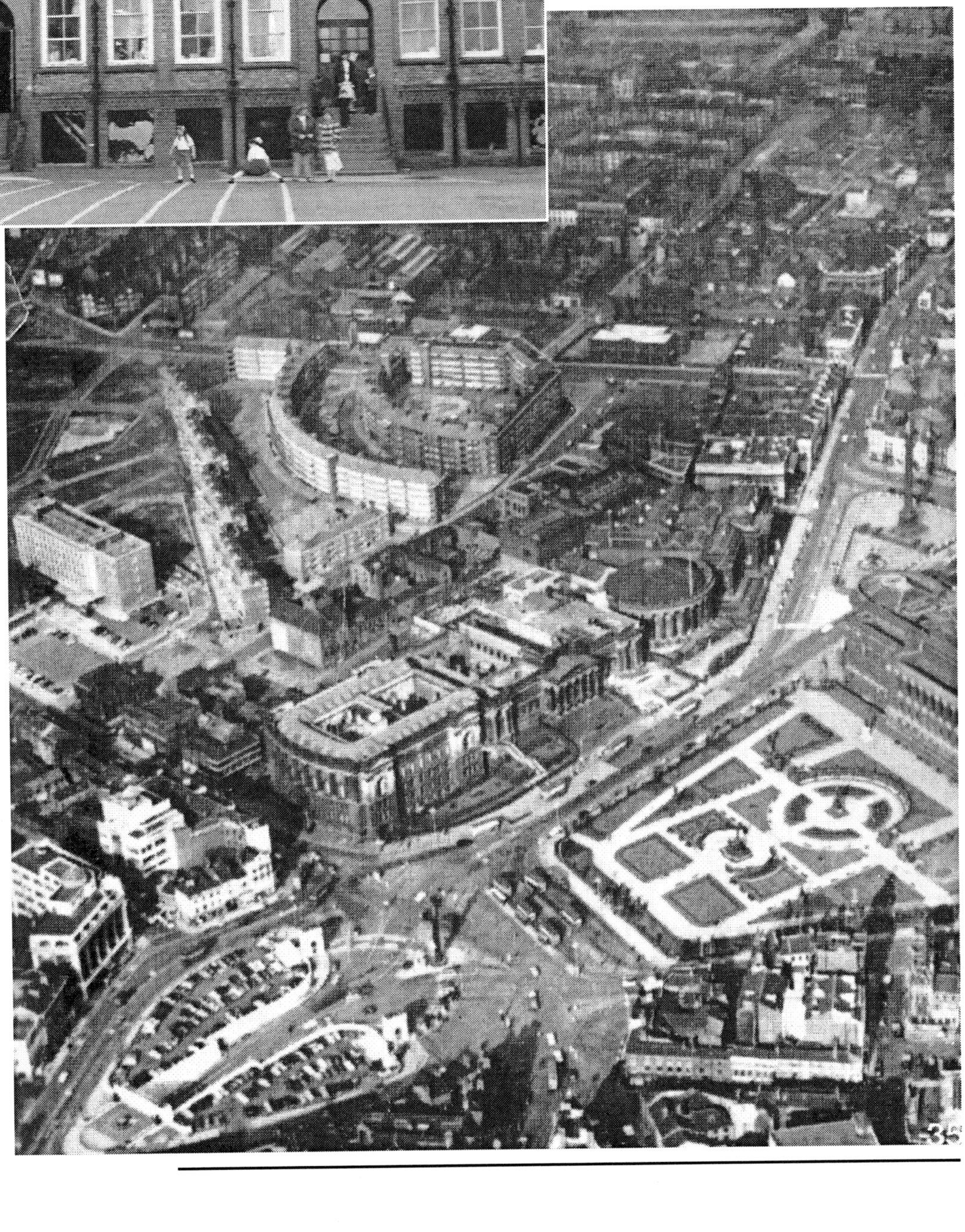

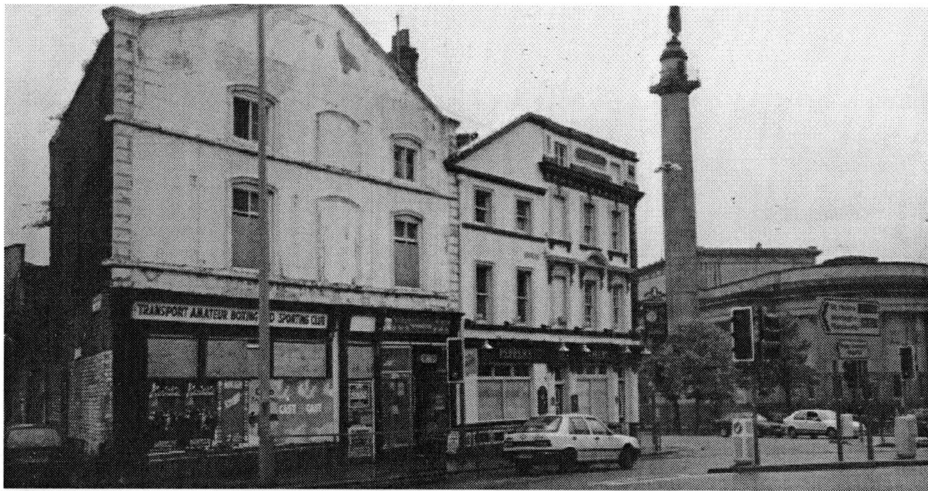

Islington 1986 looking towards Commutation Row. A well known trio of buildings which served the local residents well. Transport House boxing club, Barney's sweet shop and the County Hotel, renamed here under the nickname it was always called anyway, Peppers.

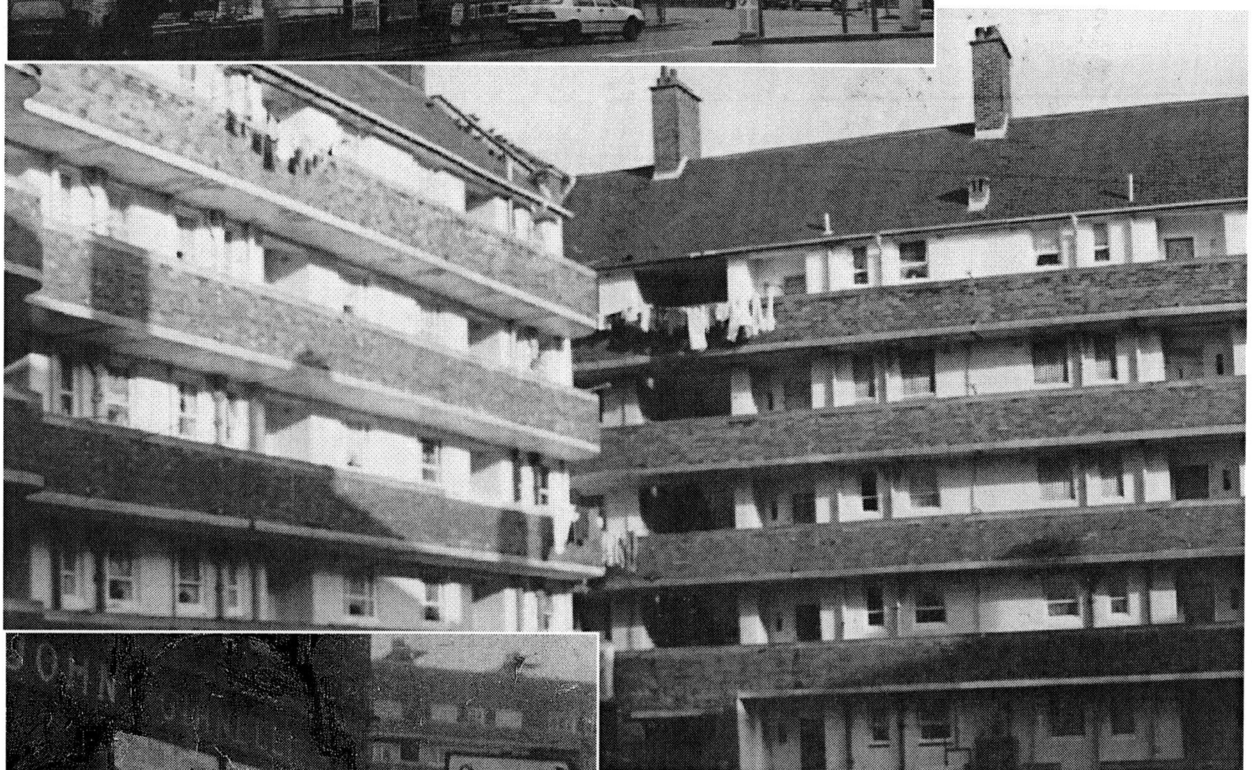

The Holy block/main Crescent block intersection (if it were a motorway) Many a game of 60 seconds took place in the staircase opening during the 1970s.

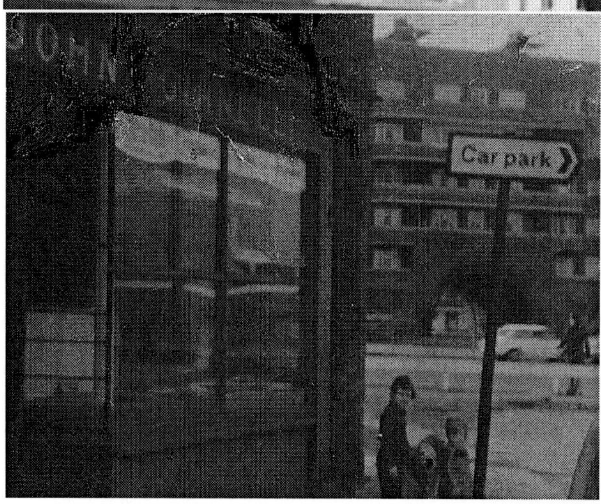

The local fish and chip shop, Gianelli's. John, Frank and Maria were local figures in the community. For 80 years they were world famous in the area as the top American showbiz stars appearing at the nearby Empire would send out for a pie in the fat or fish, chips and mushy peas.

Gerard Crescent in 1986. This view is looking towards the bottom end at Hunter Street and Gerard Close. Downe, Lionel and Cartwright House are off to the right, Thurlow House being just out of the picture.

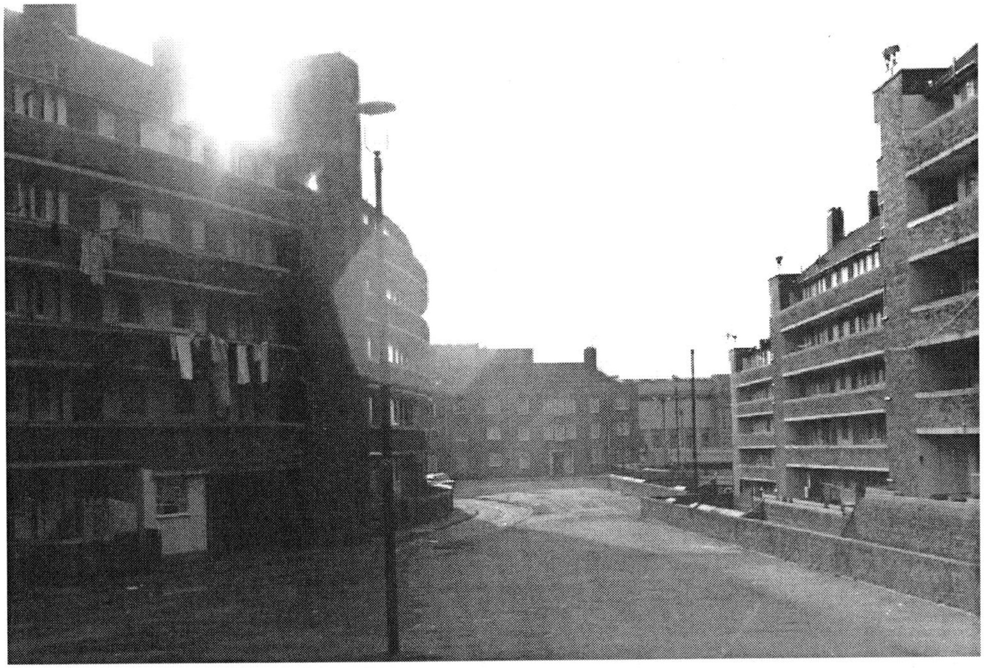

Most of the flats on the main curve of the Crescent are tinned up awaiting demolition, having been inhabited for the last time just a few short months before.

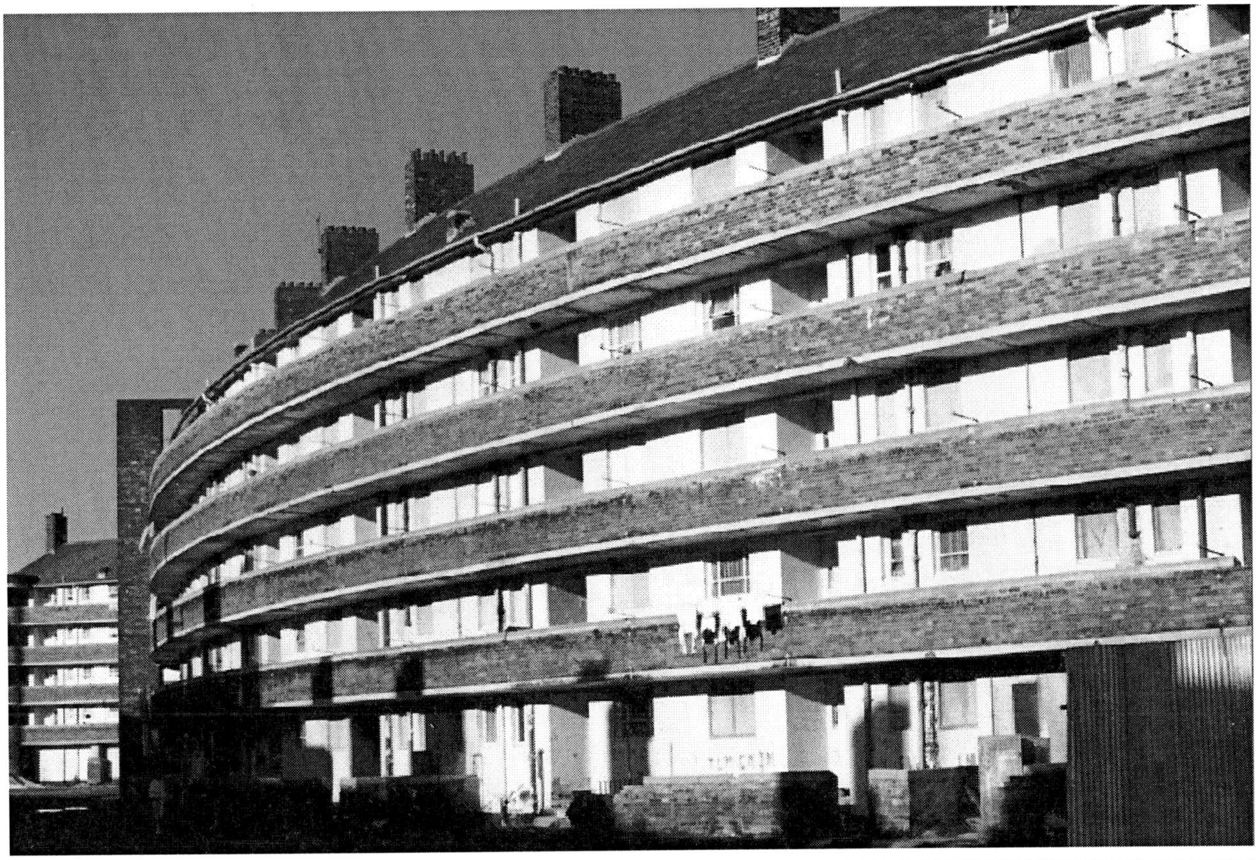

Christian Street 1986 is still a hive of activity as work starts on the new Rose Hill and Comus Street housing which will cater for some of the residents being rehoused from the development behind. The 59 Ribble to Old Roan and the L3 to Crosby proceed on their journeys as Christian Street is being used as a car park for the students of the nearby John Moores University. A George F. Knowles furniture wagon, whom were based on nearby St. Anne Street is one of the vehicles in view. .

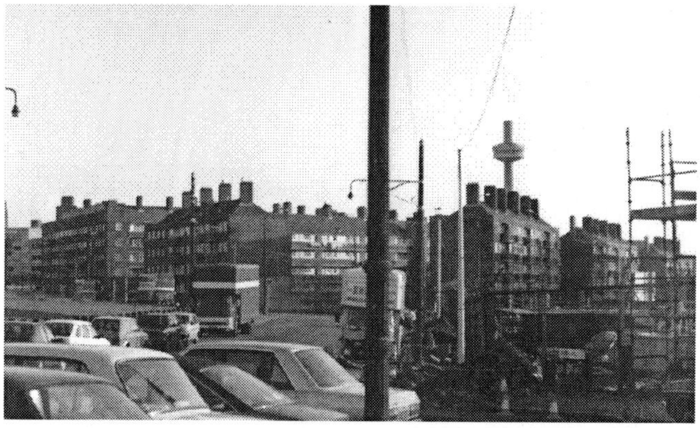

A lovely summers day, the last summer these blocks were to see.

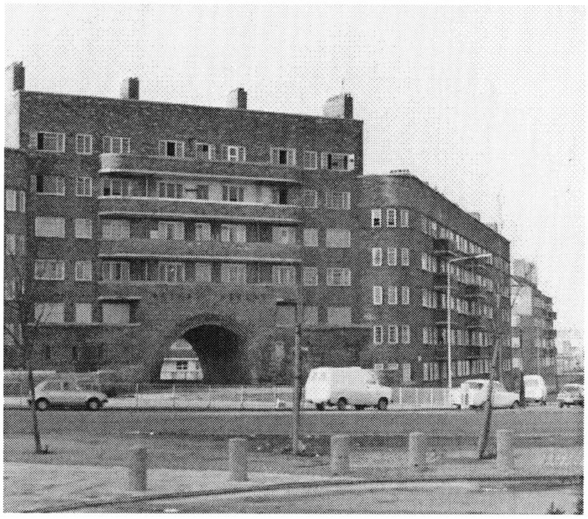

This shot is looking past the main entrance to Gerard Gardens towards the Holy block which stood facing the Pontack Public House on Christian Street. Comus Street flats are in the background.

A fine view of the vast expanse of the square with only ghostly echoes of the one time spontaneous football matches and girls skipping and playing gutters. This was one of the biggest inter war developments in the city, this part alone holding over 130 families.

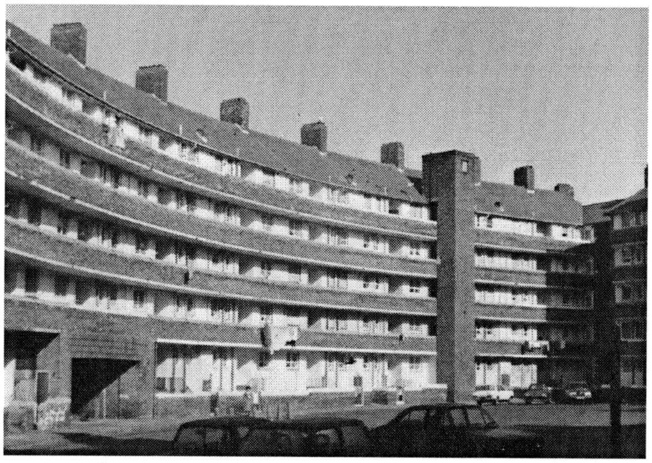

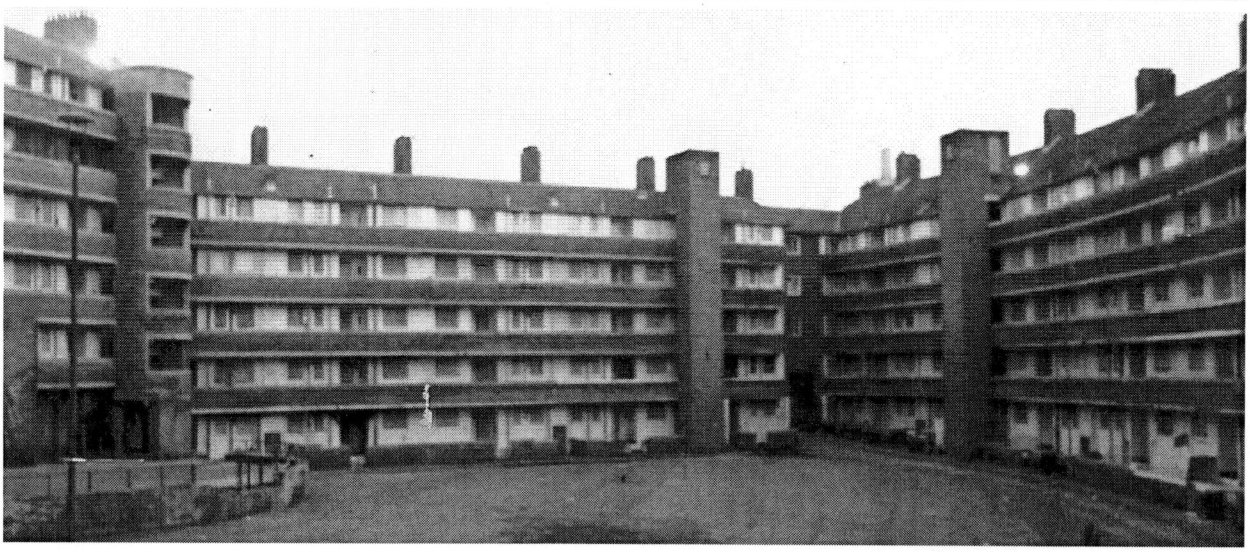

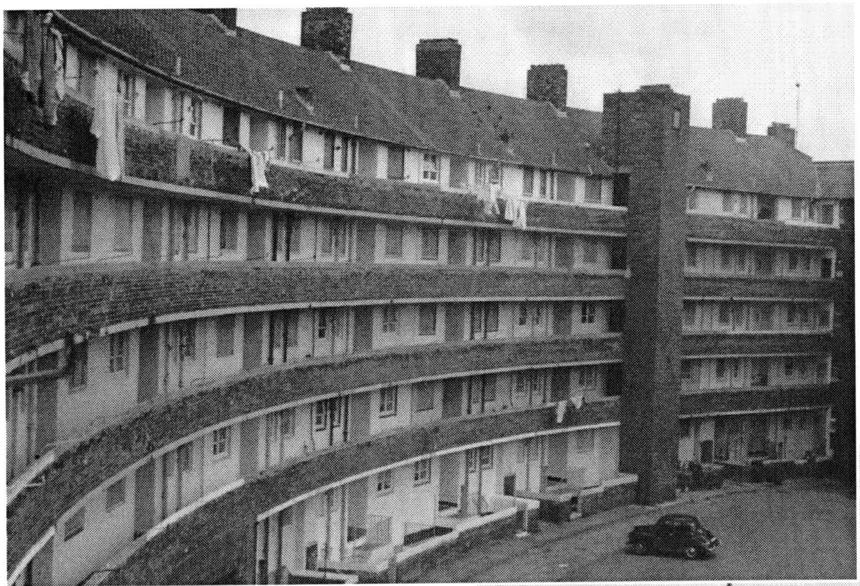

Sweeping curved landings and compact living kept people in touch with one another through close proximity living. The local community spirit was lost in spreading people far and wide and would never be quite the same again.

The new Hunter Street layout takes shape as does the plinth for the Hod Carrier memorial statue. The J.M. University can now be clearly seen in the background as the blocks bite the dust.

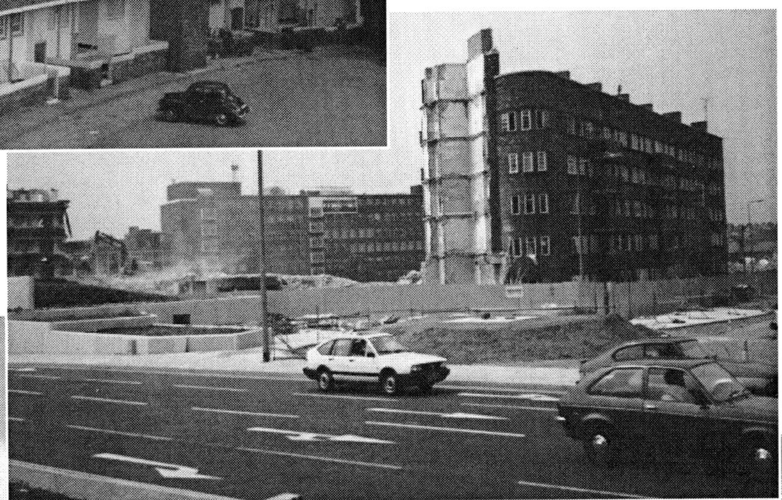

Gerard Gardens demolition in 1987. Sloyan Doyles mechanical diggers take a break for a chat.

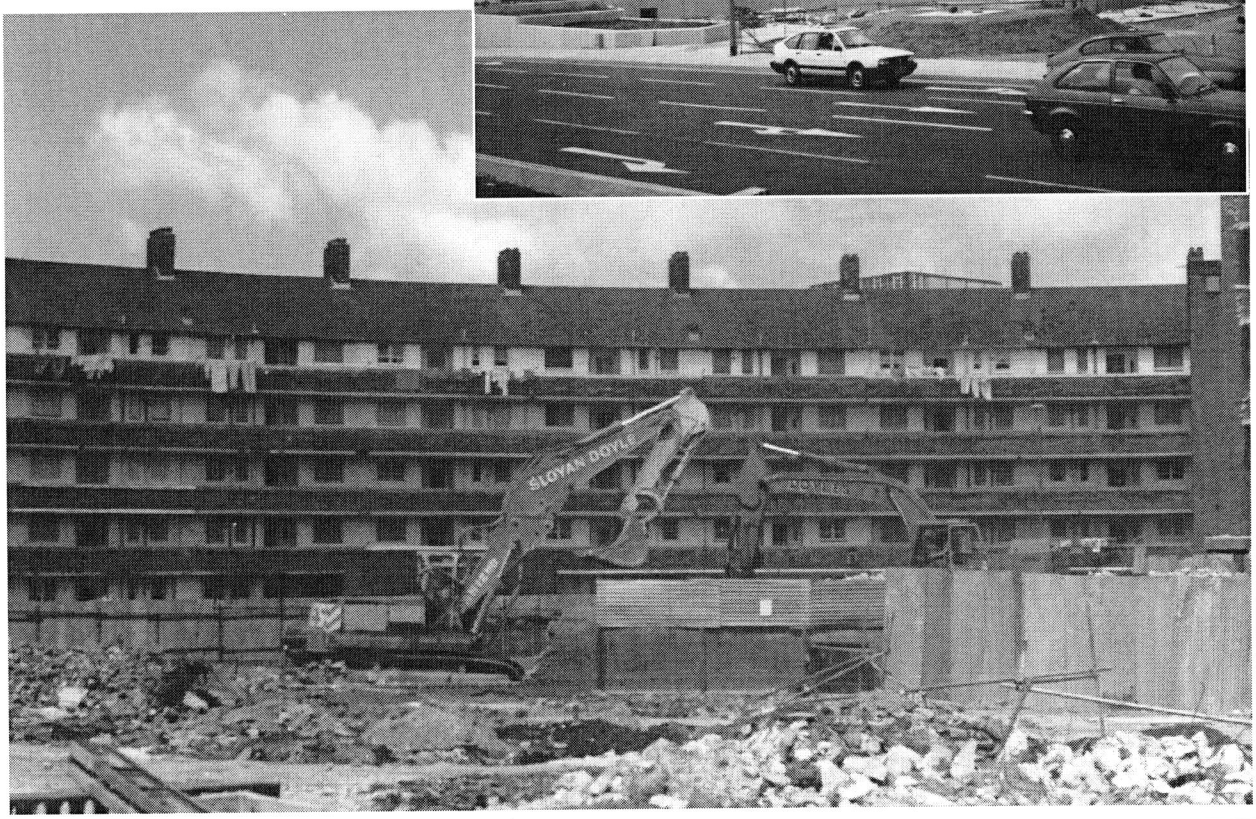

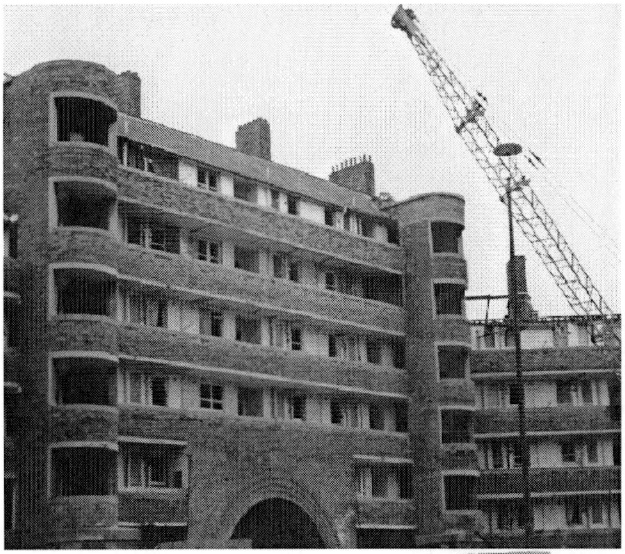

Looking as desolate as it possibly could, within a month it would be there no more.

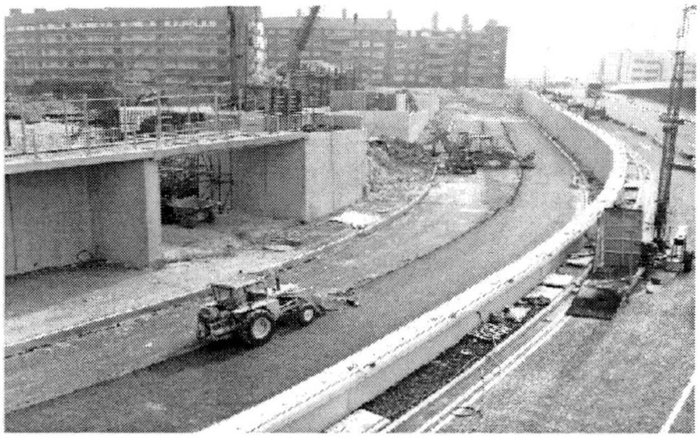

Hunter Street is widened to a six lane mini motorway to the cost of the tenement blocks and local community.

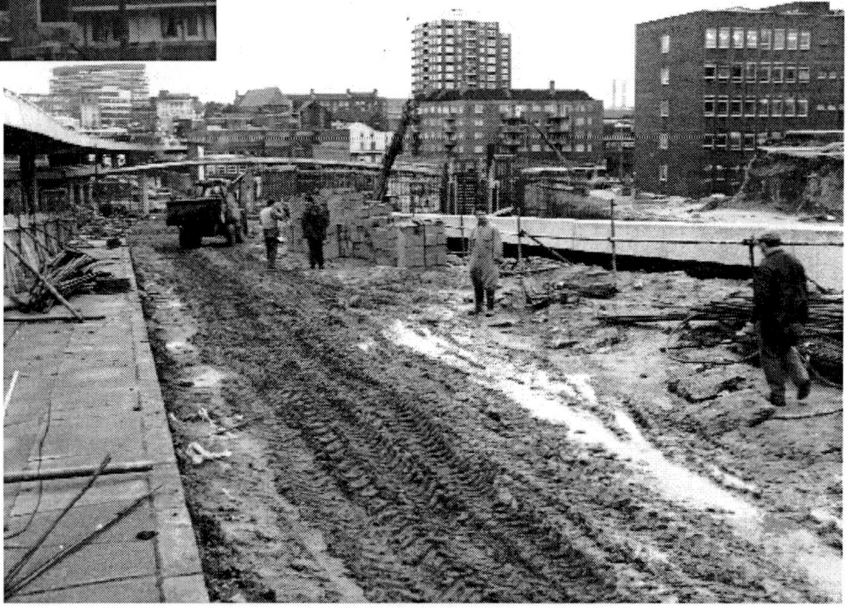

Hunter Street gone West. Many of the buildings in the distance have now gone including Fontenoy Gardens, The Coffin blocks, Holy Cross Church, The Australian Public House, The Byrom (Pie Shop) Public House and the Clarence Dock power station chimneys.

My scale model showing Gerard Gardens, Crescent and accompanying blocks from Hunter Street and from Islington.

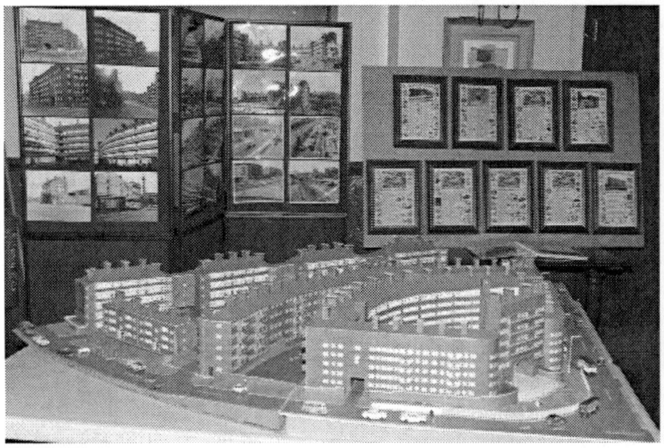

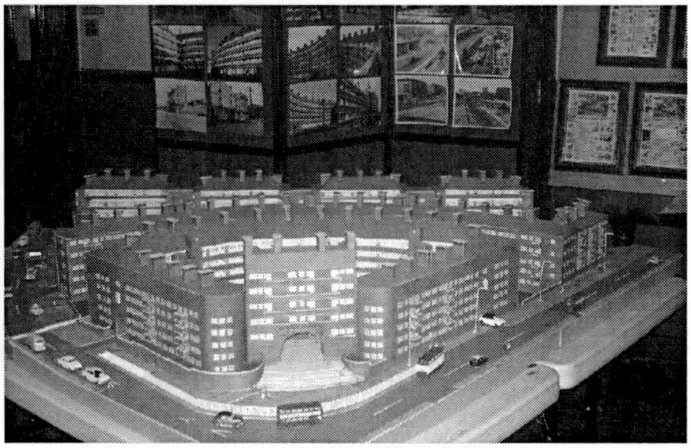

SAINT ANNE STREET/ SOHO STREET

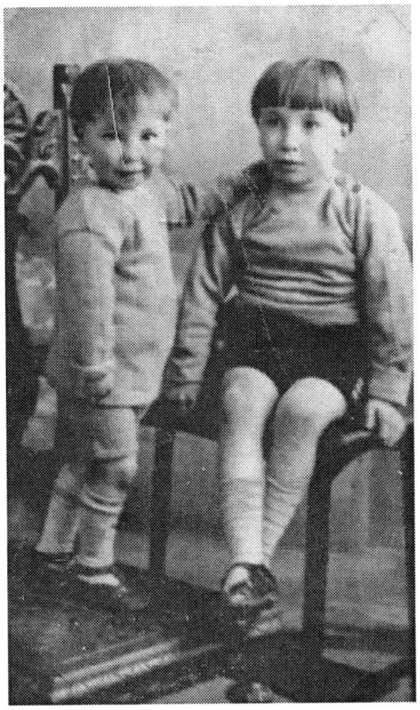

James and Joseph Fagan, taken in Jeromes, London Road in 1926. Joe, my dad, had 5 siblings in all, Elizabeth, James, Daniel, William and Francis. When this was taken they were living at No.14 House, No.3 Court, St. Anne's Terrace which was a court off St. Anne Street. His mam, my nan, Christina lived until 1983, dying just 4 days short of her 85th birthday. His dad, Daniel died in the same year of this photograph from the effects of poisoning suffered during the first world war of 1914-18.

Richmond Row was once the western end of a great thoroughfare into Scotland Road which commenced up at the Everton Water tower at Margaret Street. Lloyd Street continued westbound to Village Street and then Everton Brow before becoming Richmond Row at the junction of Fox Street. Richmond Row itself, ended at Scotland Place. Named after reformer, Charles Lennox, 3rd Duke of Richmond, the name actually lent itself to the whole area in general. Richmond fair which sold merchandise, cloth and woollens from 1787 to 1875 was the site which now houses St. Mary of the Angels Catholic church, though sadly it is now closed down. St. Anne's Church, in which, the earliest use of iron columns in England was used and from which St. Anne Street gets its name was known as St. Anne's Richmond.

Great Richmond Street still houses one of the earliest and smallest blocks of inter war tenements ever built. Containing just twenty flats, this three high 'L' shaped block hails from 1923 and its landings are of

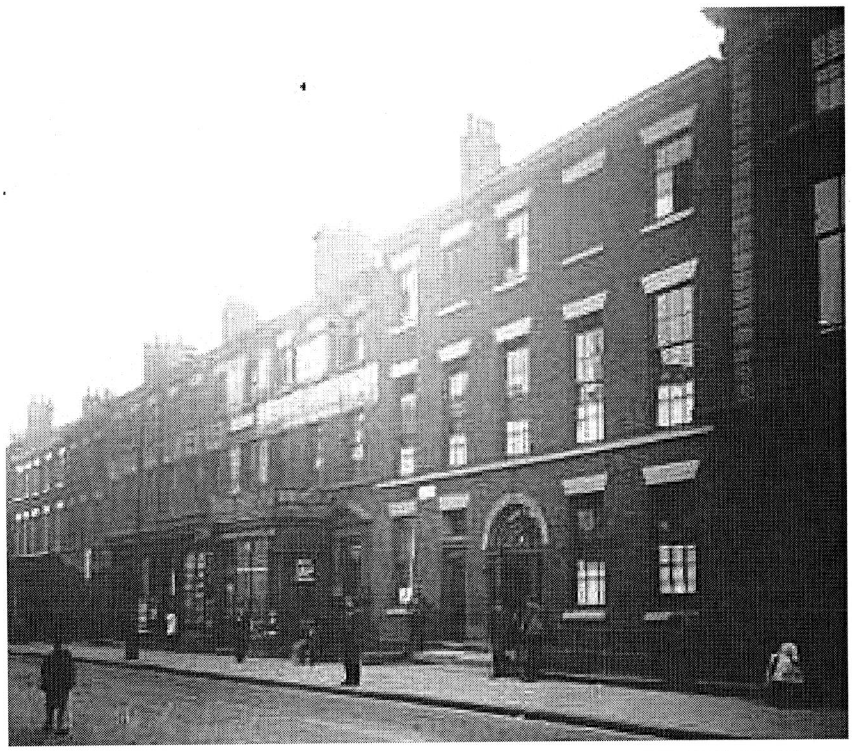

St. Anne Street summer 1925 though you wouldn't think so. A row of lodging houses, one of which is the Beresford Hotel can be seen. Originally built as Merchant Mansions, this was once a desirable wealthy area.

Looking up Roscommon Street towards the heights on Netherfield Road. The Farmers Arms Public House and the business premises of George Lowe exist on the right.

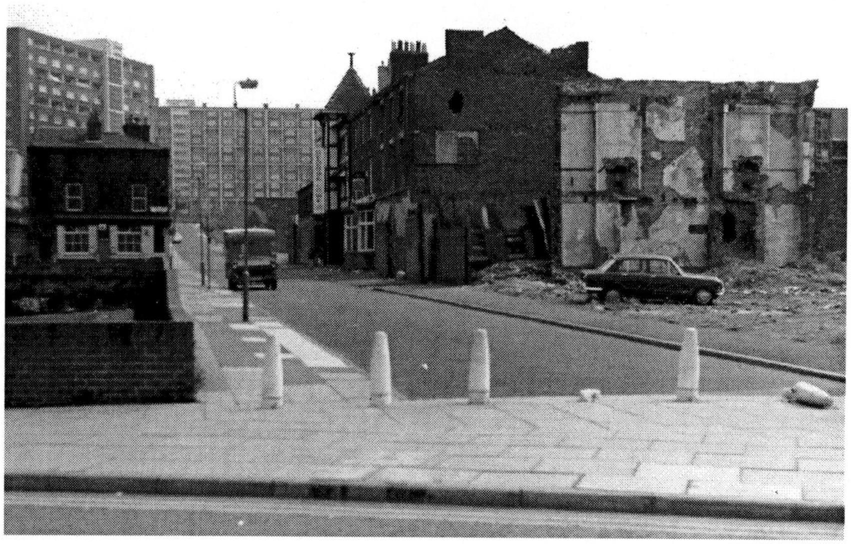

Roscommon Street from a different angle a few years later. The Cotton Picker Public House on the corner of Portland Place has been 'done up'. The School which was used by nearby St. Gregory's in the mid 1970s is in view but the one time home of Henry Morton Stanley of 'Dr Livingstone I presume' fame is just being demolished. Georges heights is the towering white block whilst two of the three blocks named after the Italian Unifists Mazzini, Garibaldi and Cavour can be seen.

the traditional wrought iron style of that era. Known locally during the 1970s as 'Ghost town' due to its quietness, they are now enjoying a 21st Century new lease of life as St. Anne's apartments. What's the difference between a flat and an apartment one might ask. If I were cynical, I'd say about £80,000. Another example of what could have been achieved with a bit of foresight and imagination now that inner city, downtown living is back in vogue.

On the south side of Richmond Row stands Birkett Street, once home to a small development of tenement blocks. Built in a digital number two shape, these four high blocks were built between 1935 and 1937

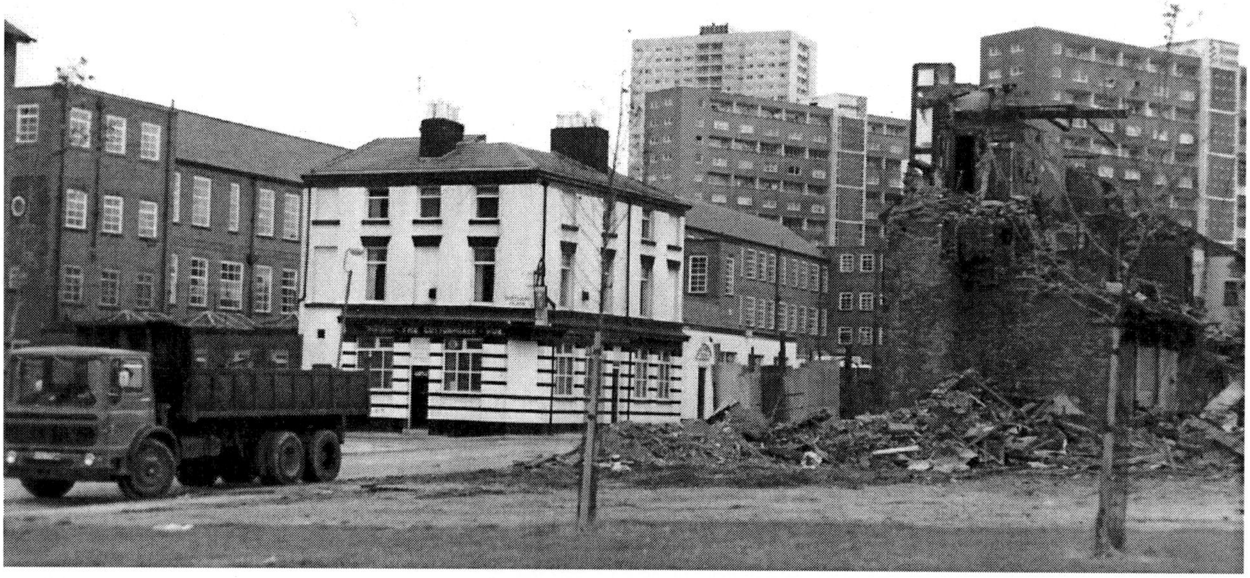

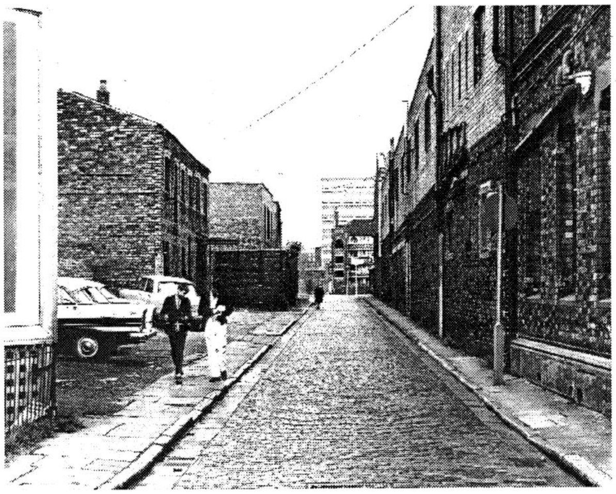

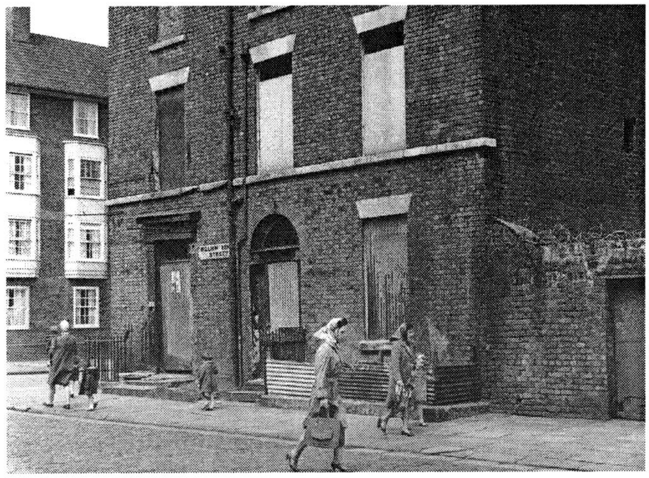

Two mid 60s views of Birkett Street tenement though you'll have to look hard on the first picture. Looking East past Keisers Clock tower and Orwell Engineering, the staircase end is just in view. The other photo shows the back of the tennies from William Henry Street, the doss house on the corner has long since gone.

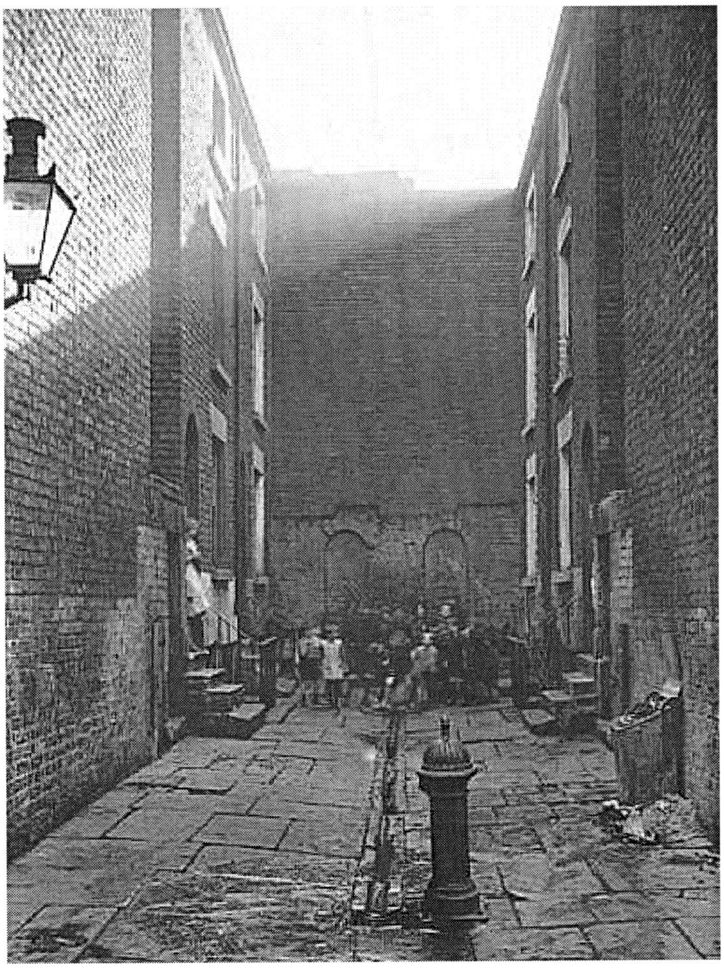

on the site of commercial premises which once stood on Atkinson Street, Scarlet Street and Tessera Place. Across the way were such fine sounding addresses as Drinkwater Gardens and Fletchers Gardens but in reality this was a slum ridden area. Even during the 1970s there were a lot of vacant premises such as those

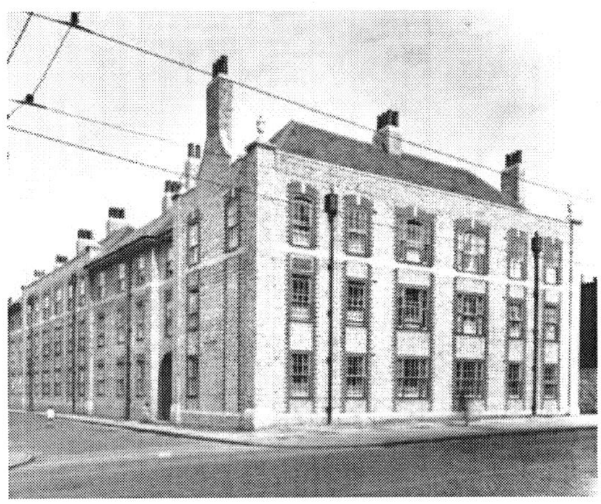

Great Richmond Street tenements pictured here upon completion are still going strong today as private apartments.

No.2 Court Gomer Street in 1933 showing what it was like to live in this area just prior to its demolition for the building of the four squares

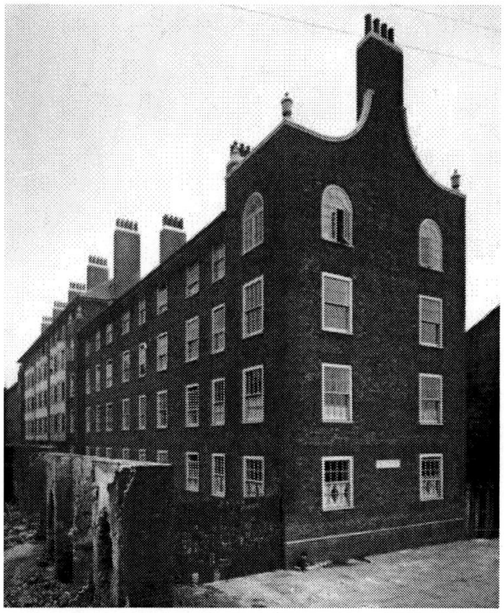

1933. This is the first block of 44 new flats in the Queen Anne Street area.

of Pitt & Scott, Full Swing and Hertz van hire as well as a smattering of scrap iron dealers. The crime here is that there was no need to raze these blocks or their neighbouring 'mother' blocks, the four squares as nothing has ever been built on their site and even the landscaping is so harsh and uneven that it's unusable.

The area to the East of St. Anne Street was cleared of slums in the early 1930s. The first block of tenements in this area was completed in 1933 at Queen Anne Street, replacing squalid courts in Torbock Street and Back Queen Anne Street. By 1935, eight oblong rows of flats, some four high, some five had been built to form what were to become known locally as the four squares. A far cry from the dilapidated dimly lit cellar dwellings that once existed in Gomer Street and Travers Street. Holly Street tenements built in 1923, at the time of the Great Richmond Street development linked the four squares area with the Gerard Crescent complex. Geographically, it ran between both sets of flats from St Anne Street down to Christian Street and when demolished in 1969, many residents found their way to one or the other of the aforementioned blocks. Starting life on the site of an old brewery, of which there were a number in the area, they were an improvement on the pre 1st world war dwellings from a decade earlier which they faced across Holly Street.

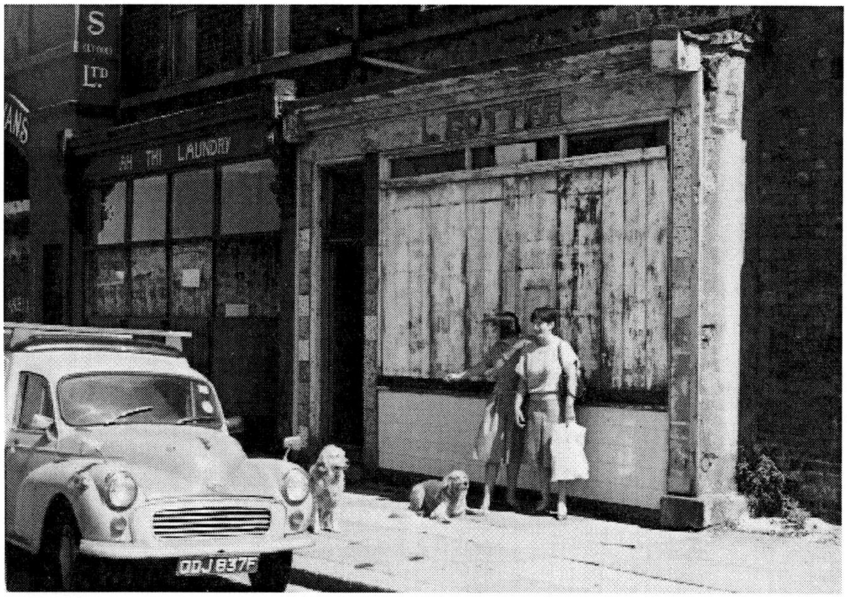

The Ah Thi Laundry owned by Kit who also had a chippy on nearby Everton Brow. His chippy and Railo's sweet shop serviced the kids of the Friary and St. Gregs schools for years over. Cotters is also pictured, scene of many a basin head haircut throughout its life. This is Soho Street in the early 1980s.

Due to the gradient of Holly Street, these are one of only two blocks in Liverpool that contravened the building regulations at the time, whereby a sixth floor was allowed as the top end of the street had a block whose ground floor flats were actually below street level. These tenements were situated between Gaskell's commercial premises and the Myrtle Vaults public house which stood at the bottom of the street at its junction with Christian Street. Holly Street

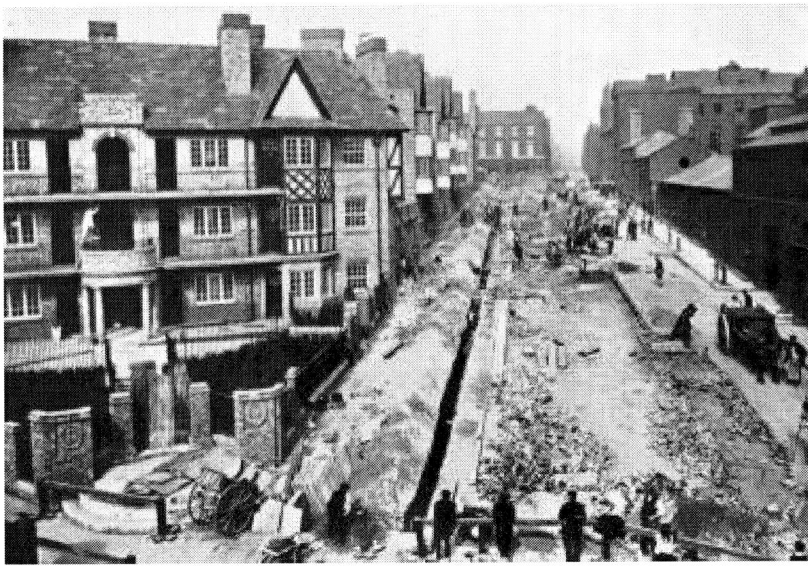

was once actually called Myrtle Street from which the pub got its name and the flats fronted onto Myrtle View. These tennies which contained just 39 flats were demolished to make way for St. Anne Street police headquarters prior to the new 'A' Division in Canning Place.

The newly completed flats are shown here in 1914 as Holly Street is widened. The brewery on the right would be demolished within the decade to be replaced by a block of tenements.

Holly Street tenements that fronted onto the abolished Myrtle View and Christian Street were built in 1923 before falling victim to redevelopment of the area themselves in 1969. Although the land they were on was not in direct conflict with the building of the new Police Station, it lay dormant for many years until part of St. Joseph's Crescent was built on it in 1987.

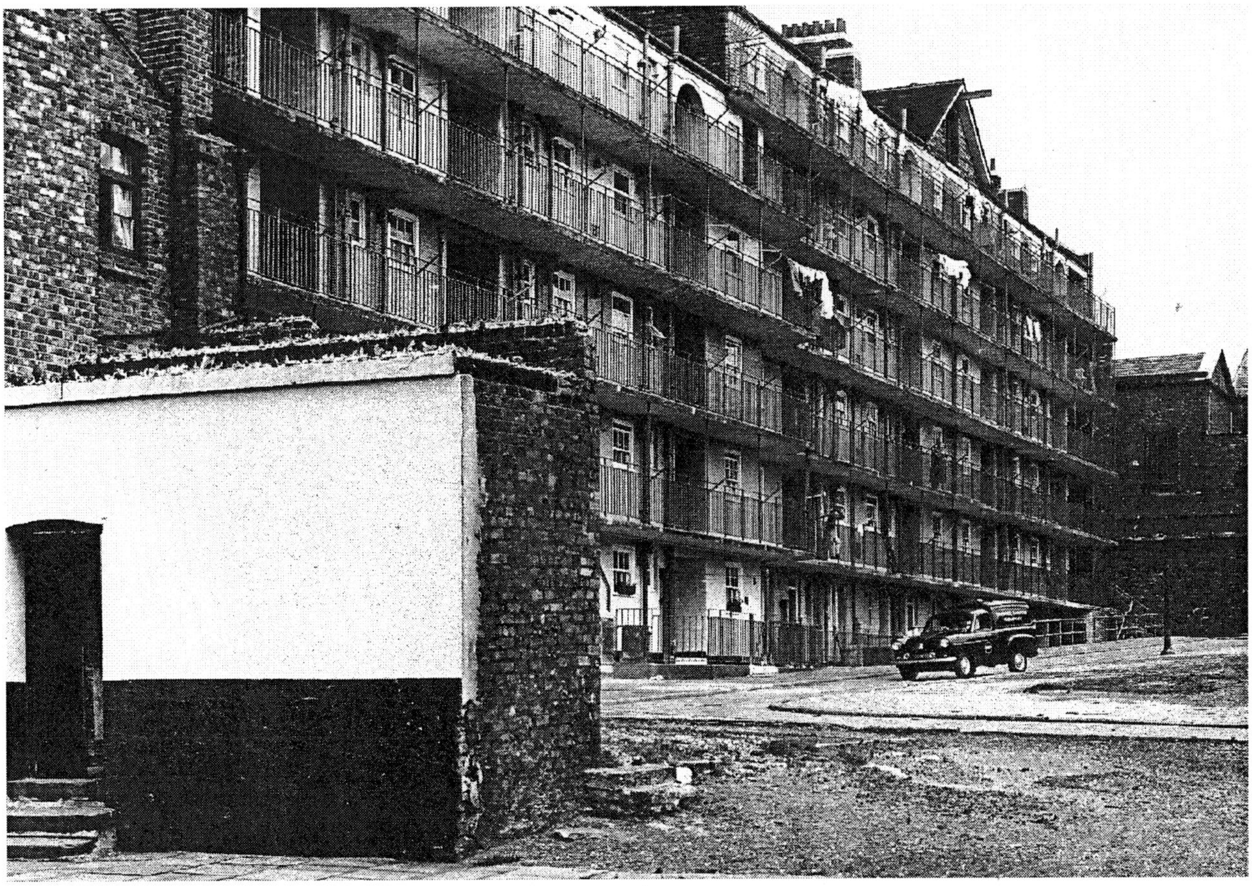

EAST OF THE CITY CENTRE

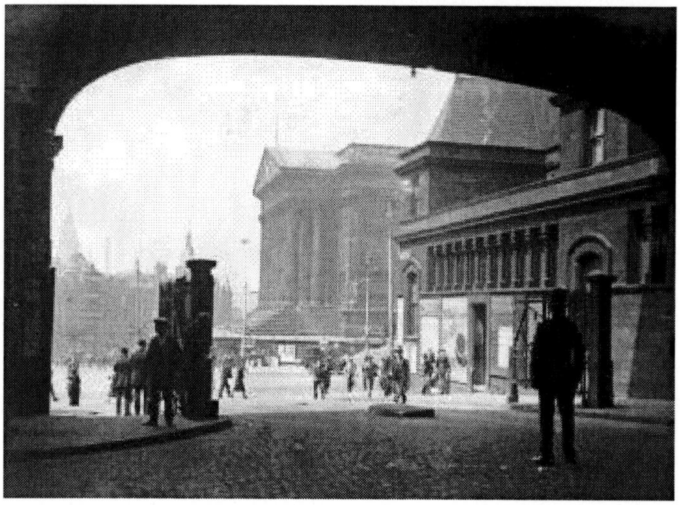

A 1920s view from the original arched entrance to Lime Street station which was Gloucester Street, looking towards the South Portico of St. George's Hall

COPPERAS HILL

Immediately to the rear of the London North Western Railway Station at Lime Street stood a labyrinth of streets containing commercial premises interspersed with numerous courts and cellar dwellings in1920s Liverpool. The North End and South End abattoirs stood at either end of Trowbridge Street and there were no fewer than four hide stores and markets on St. Andrew Street and Gill Street which dated back to the mid 1840s. Other property included a smelting works, jam factory, vehicle maintenance yards and a flour mill which existed between Brownlow Hill and Copperas Hill.

Situated off Norton Street linking the four squares area with that of the Bullring, here is a 1926 view across a cobbled Kempston Street. Very different from how it looks now

Copperas Hill actually got its name from the copperas works on the hill which was closed down by the council when its owner, Richard

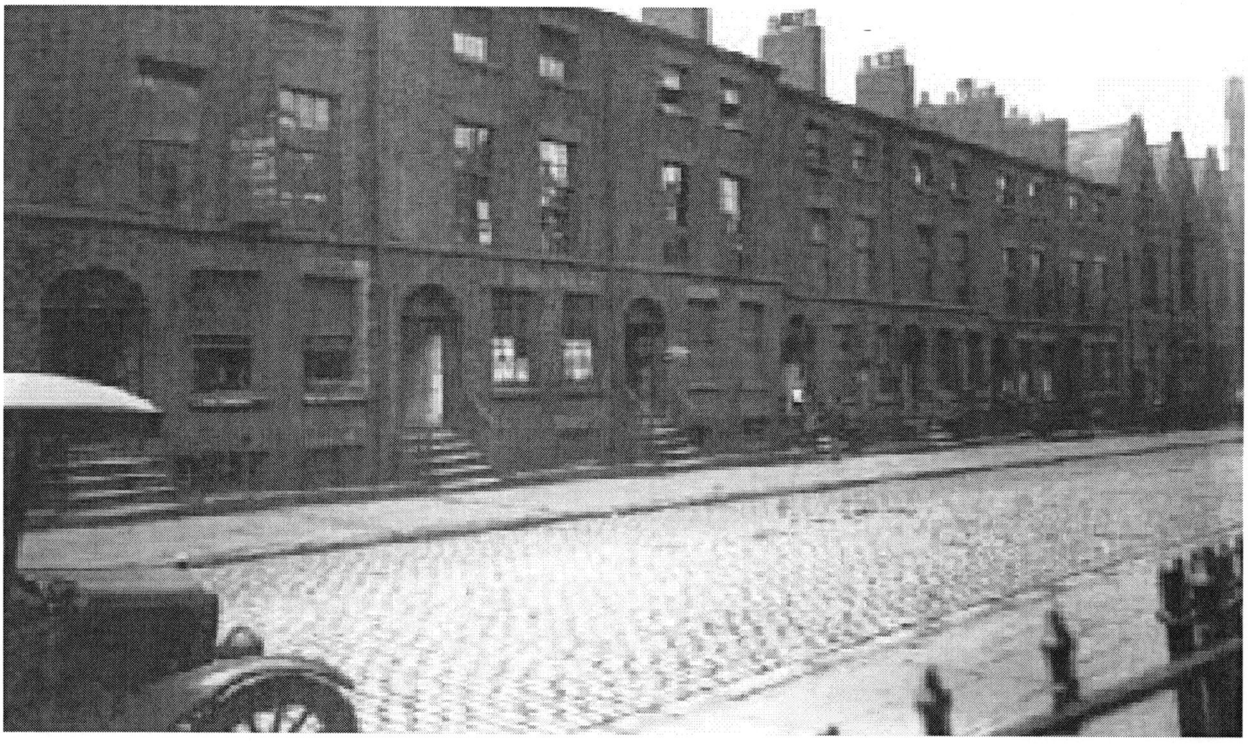

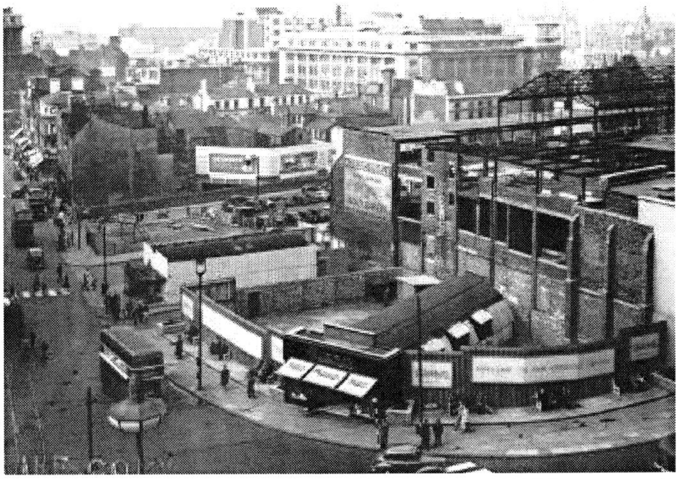

Hughes who was Mayor of Liverpool in 1756 was prosecuted because of the foul smells it emitted. In 1933 much of the aforementioned property was demolished to allow for the construction of St. Andrews Gardens. These became known as the Bullring due to the lands association with bulls having been driven through the area to the abattoirs and because of the bullring shape part of the tenement development was it was given in commemoration.

September 1952 and the war torn city centre is still awaiting attention on the corner of Ranelagh Street facing Lewis's store. Temporary shops were opened in the interim period and a tunnel was made to access other retail premises. Kumar Brothers building would soon be built here which currently lays empty, save for a row of individual shops at ground floor level.

A public health exhibition was held at George Henry Lee's department store in Liverpool city centre from 13th-18th May 1935, showcasing a model of these new flats which were constructed like many, because of the growing residential population of the area in unacceptable living conditions. Just over a month later on 21st June, on the same day as that of Gerard Gardens, the foundation stone was laid for St. Andrew's Gardens by the Rt Honourable Sir Kingsley Wood MP, Minister for Health.

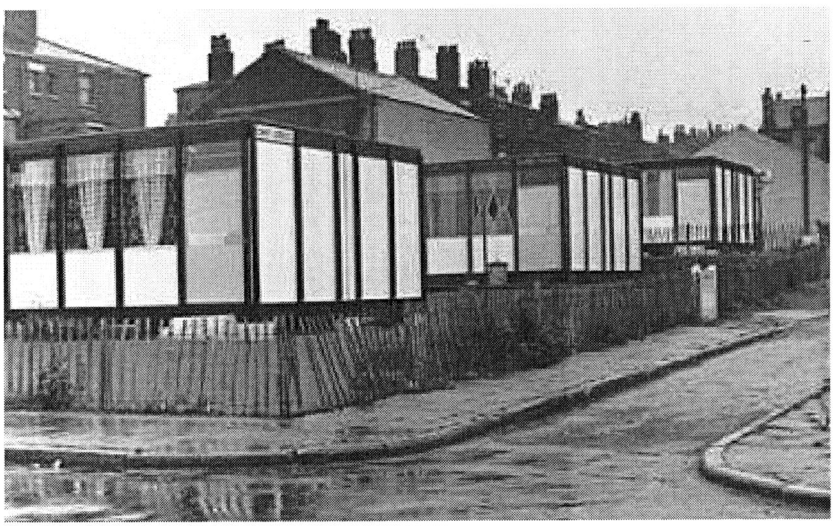

Croft Street in 1967. These prefabs were just off Prescot Street facing where the hospital is now situated. Belle Vale in the South East of the city housed Britain's largest prefab community of affordable and quick low level housing required

One block consisted of the bullring/horseshoe shape, rather like that of the Britz estate in Berlin, Germany which Sir Lancelot Keay was a known fan of. To the south of the railway cutting which lead into Lime Street terminus were three separate oblong blocks on Gill Street, St.Andrew Street and Trowbridge Street. These were just a stones throw from the old Liverpool workhouse which stood on the site which is now occupied by the Metropolitan Cathedral of Christ the King. These three blocks were razed during the citywide demolition of such housing in the mid 1980s but the bullring part itself was sold to Riverside Housing who renovated them into student accommodation offering apartments ranging from two to six bedrooms.

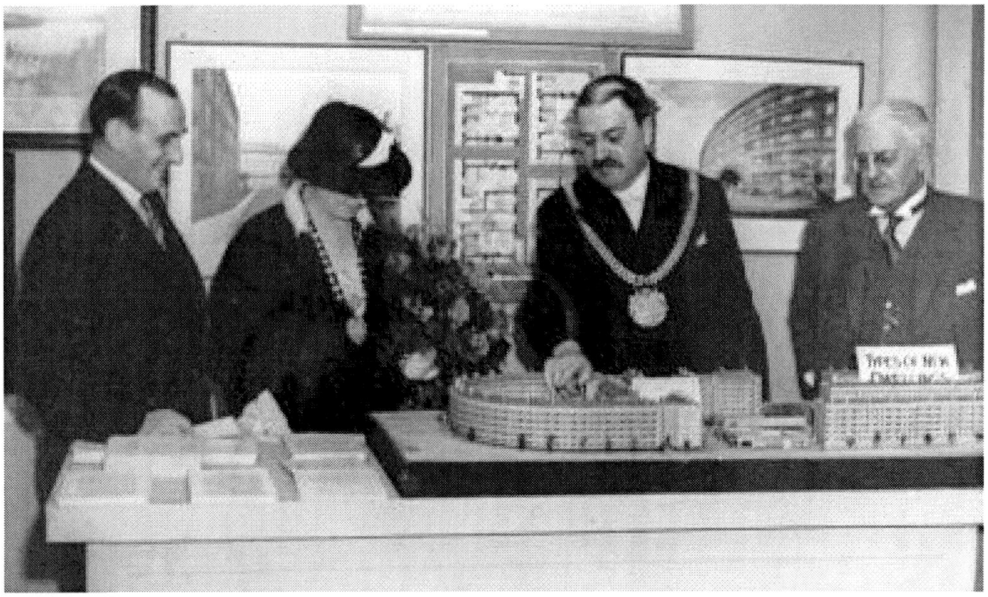

The Lord Mayor and Councillors peruse a model of the 312 new flats called St. Andrews Gardens. The venue is George Henry Lee's store which hosted the Public Health Exhibition from 13th to 18th May 1935.

A view of the brand spanking newly opened St. Andrews Gardens in May 1935. Children of the new inhabitants try out the witches hat in their new playground.

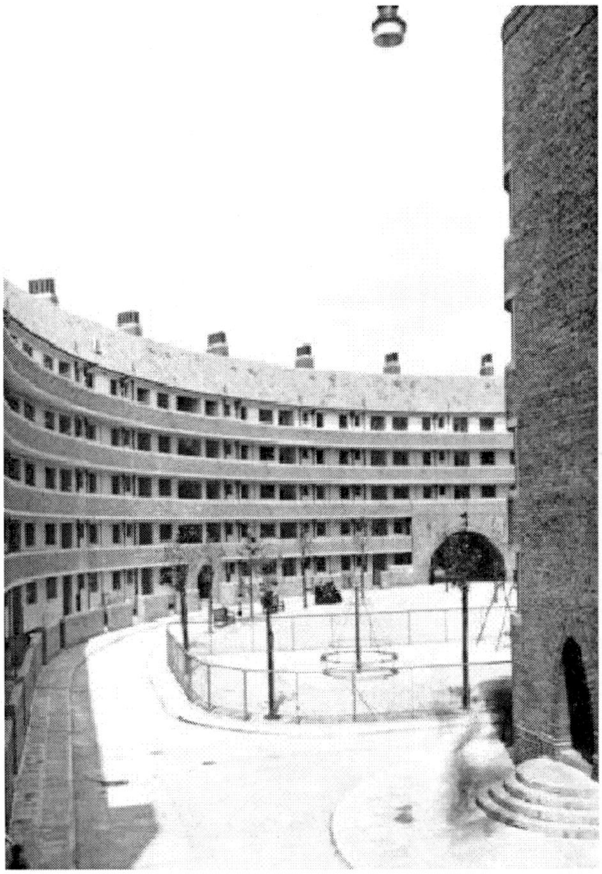

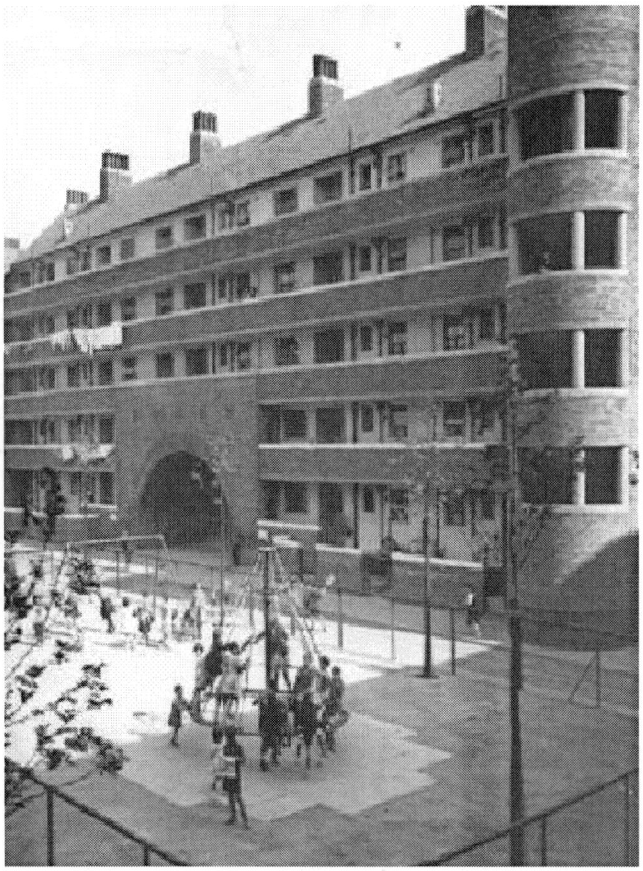

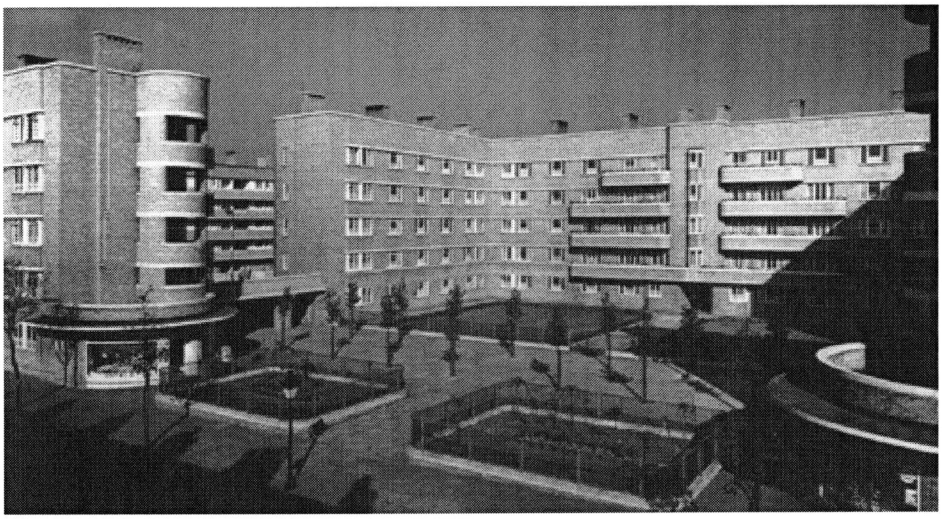

A mid 1960s view of Myrtle Gardens from nearby Entwistle Heights which also shows the construction of the new Catholic Cathedral. Also shown here is the central courtyard with the curved stairwells above the integral shops.

EDGE HILL

Myrtle Gardens opened in 1936 consisting of 344 flats built on the site of the original Botanic Gardens, the principal courtyard being on the site of the Church of the Holy Innocents which served the accompanying Liverpool Orphanage asylum which flanked it. Featured in the 1938 Liverpool Corporation documentary film 'Homes for Workers', City Architect, Lancelot Keay and a happy resident tell of life in these new blocks and how it's luxury compared to what existed before them. Demonstrating the gas hob, communal ironing facilities and showing the children's playground amongst other things, it is clear that all are proud of their achievements. These tenements fronted onto Crown Street at its junction with Myrtle Street, a sister block was also built to its south which backed onto

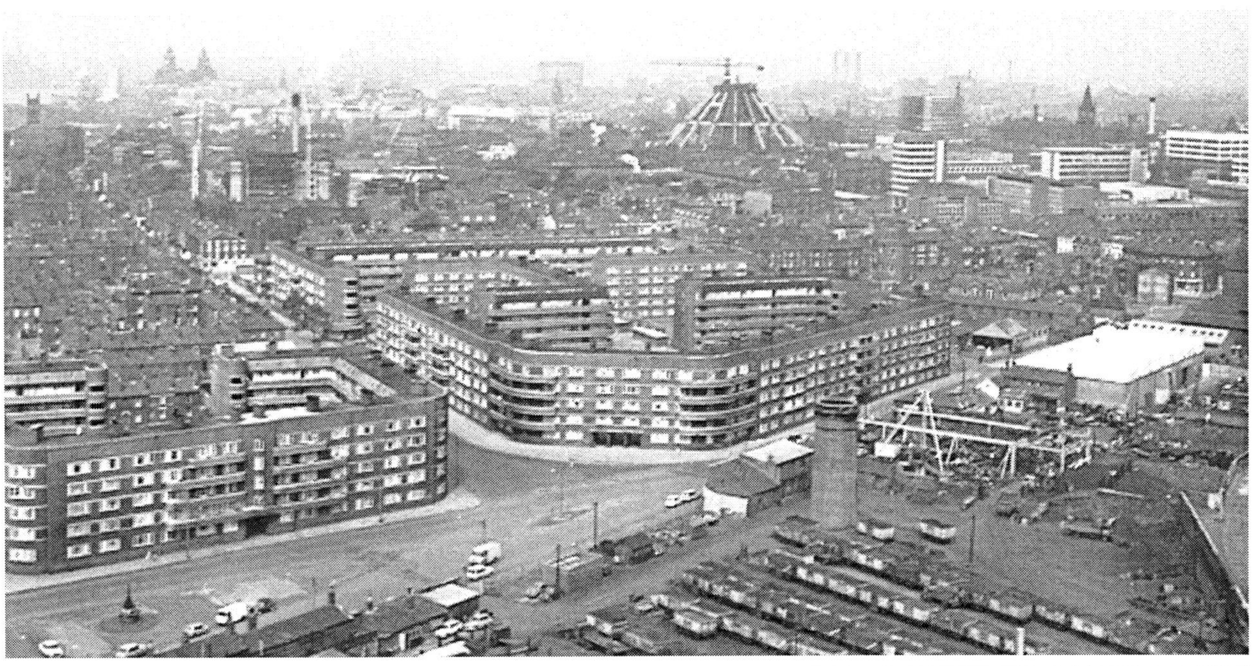

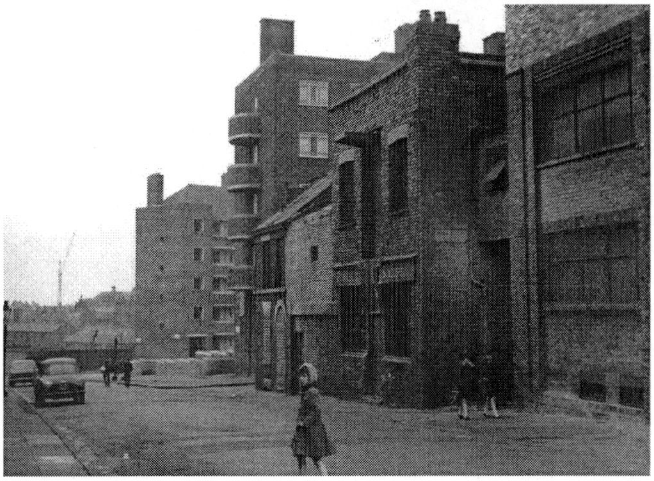

Cardwell Street looking past Back Sidney Place towards the council tenements in 1968.

Faulkner Street following the clearance of many ramshackle properties on Date Street, Citron Street, Palm Street and Almond Street.

The main structure of Myrtle Gardens was demolished in the 1980s, the blocks on Melville Place surviving to be sold off to Barrett's who converted them into student accommodation renamed Minster Court. To the East side of Smithdown Lane stood a further number of blocks on a triangular piece of land bounded by Crown Street, Irvine Street and Overbury Street. In this area, some of the older streets such as Troughton Street, Squires Street, Holt Street and Lissant Street which traversed Overbury Street were sacrificed for these blocks whilst others such as Cardwell Street and Lovat Street survived. Likewise, Edge Vale and Myers Street were cleared of industrial premises and were built on but Sidney Place was spared.

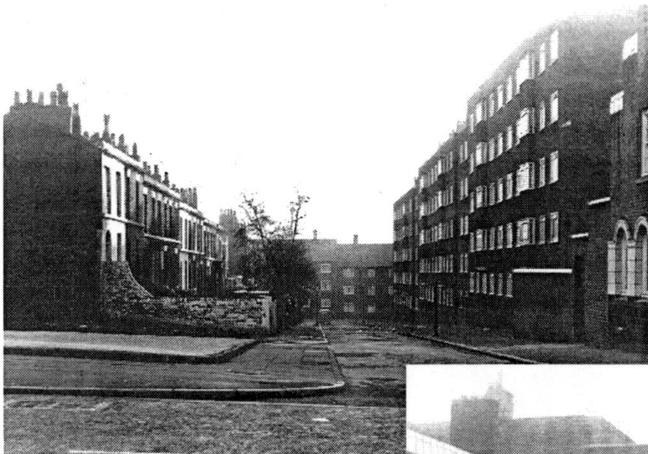

This was taken on 15th January 1968. Looking South down Sidney Place from its junction with Grinfield Street in Edge Hill, Liverpool 7.

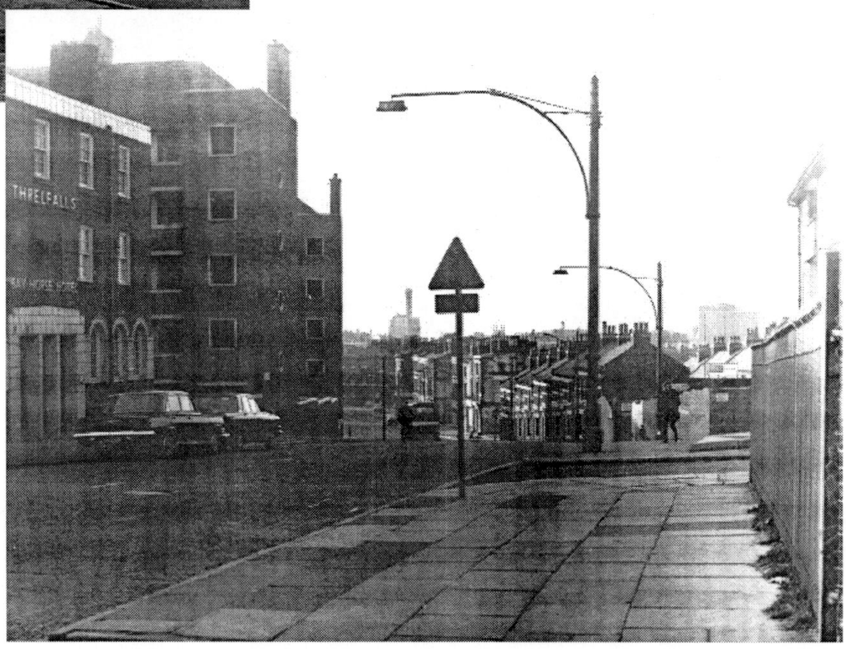

The 4th March 1968 and Grinfield Street looking Westwards towards the city. The Bay Horse Hotel is on the left serving as the local Public House to the tenement residents whilst Big Ben scaffolding Company is on the junction of Mason Street.

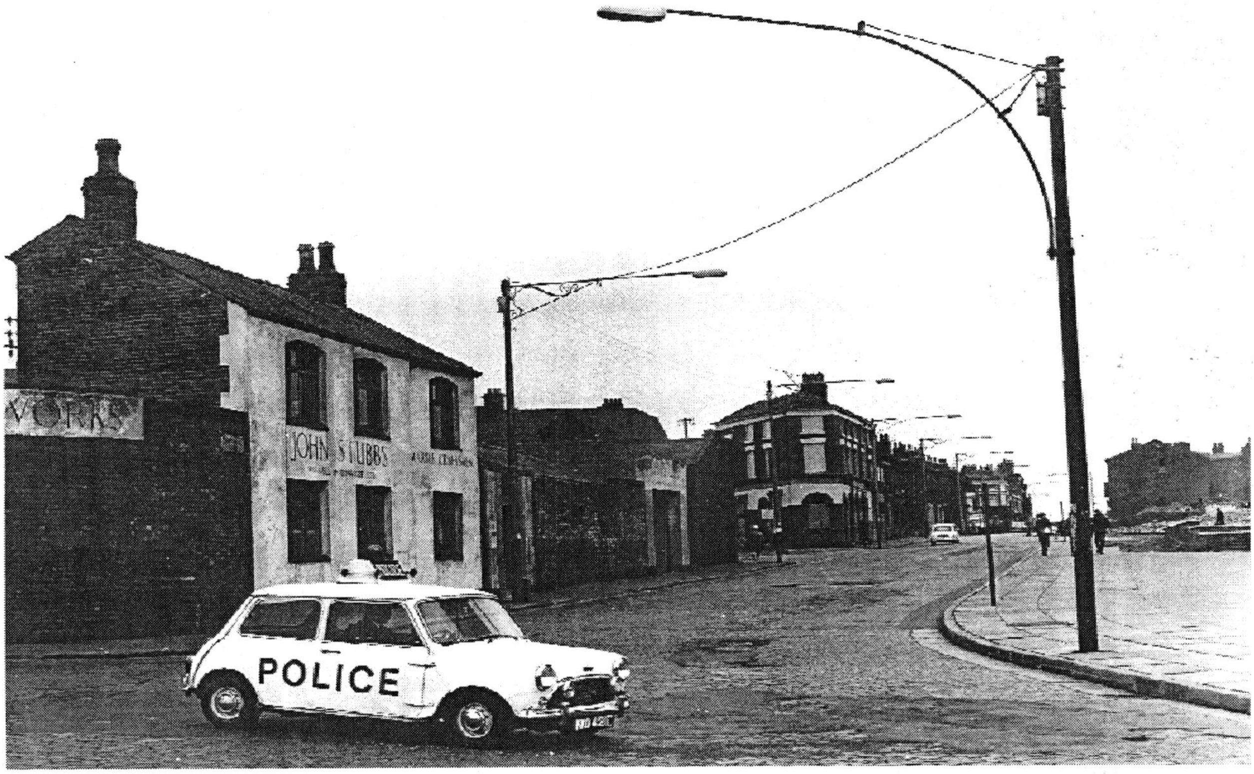

The Phoenix and the Sefton Public Houses were in the Chatsworth Street and Portwood Street clearance area and as such were subject to Compulsory purchase orders. Entwistle Heights were newly constructed on Smithdown Lane off Upper Parliament Street when pictured here in March 1965.

Smithdown Lane at its junction with Aigburth Street. John Stubbs marble craftsmen works takes up most of this corner in 1968 as a new E Reg Police Mini Cooper S patrols.

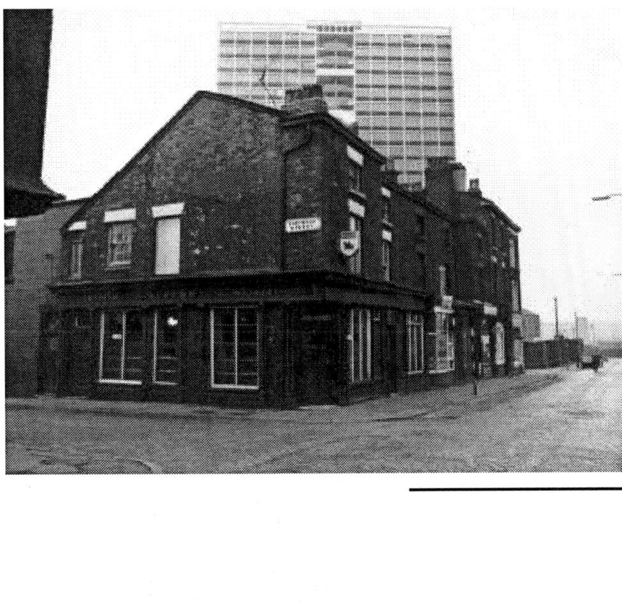

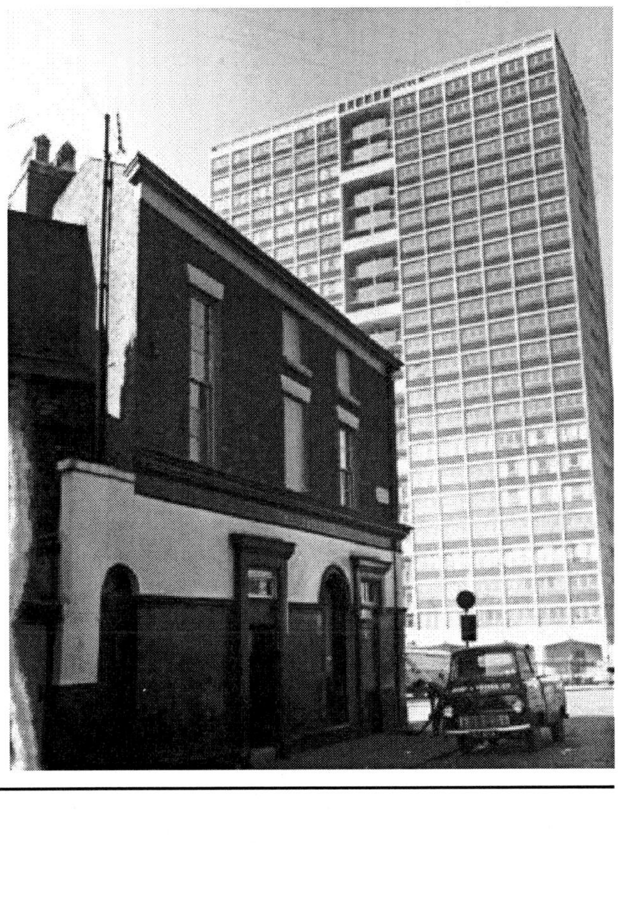

WAVERTREE

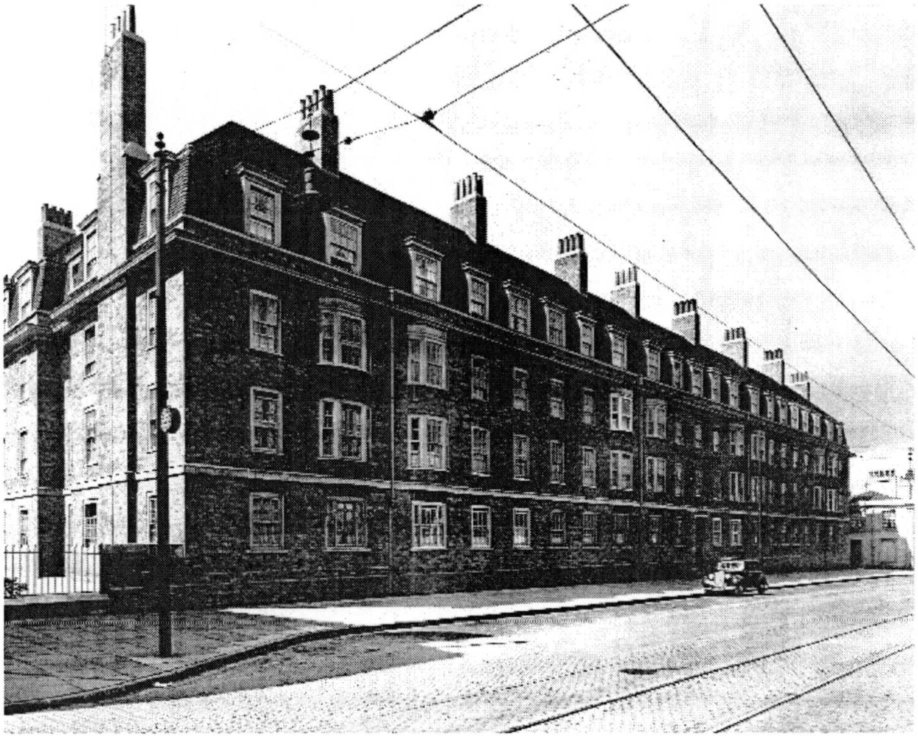

The only tenement blocks in the Liverpool 15 district were built in 1935 on the site of Anderton Square which once housed the original Wavertree Police station facing the lock up. Wavertree Gardens, flanked by the grand sounding Paradise Gardens and Rose Villas was a somewhat unusual location for working class dwellings in the village type setting that Wavertree Garden suburb was. Principally on the High Street surrounded by a number of fine listed buildings, these blocks back onto Wavertree Playground, host of the annual Liverpool Show, known to all as the 'Mystery' because it was donated to the city by an unknown benefactor.

Nearby Picton Road is named after Architect and local historian Sir James Allanson Picton, designer and builder of Italian influenced office blocks in Castle Street, Chapel Street and Dale Street. Just to the East of these tenements is the Picton clock tower which was built in 1884 as a memorial to Picton's wife, Sarah Pooley. The first public building in Liverpool to use electric lighting was in fact the PictonLibrary in William Brown Street which was the first purpose built public library in Great Britain. Wavertree was also host to the smallest house in England, situated at 95 High Street. At just 14 x 6 feet, in 1952 it was incorporated into part of the neighbouring Cock and Bottle Public House.

Wavertree Gardens were eventually sold by Liverpool City Council to London Company, Direct Build for refurbishment of the 72 flats into

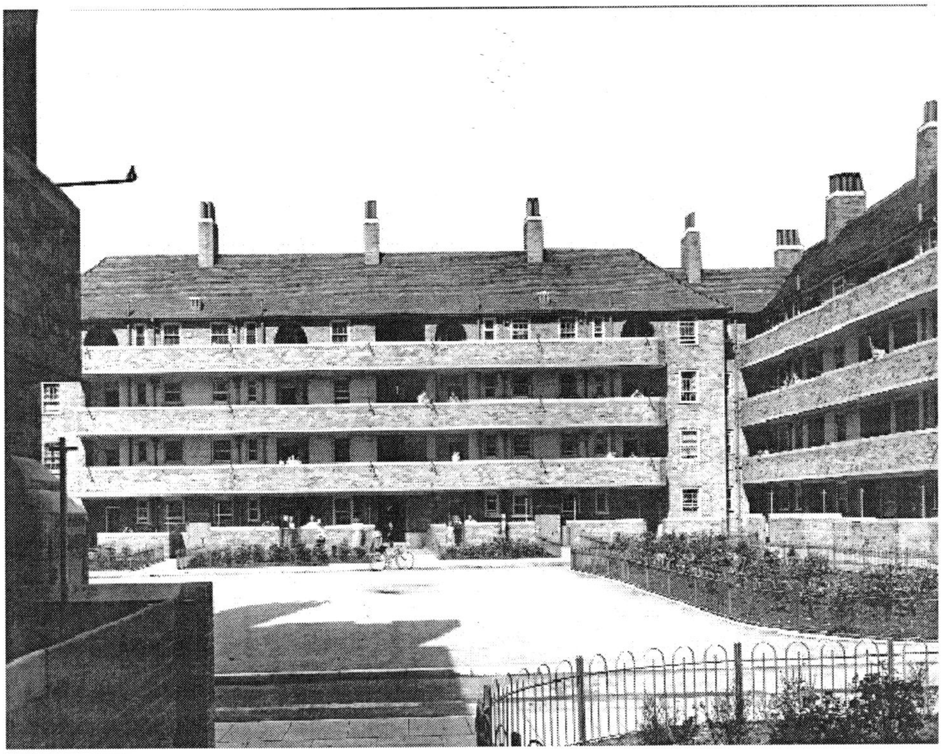

what is now an electronically gated secure block renamed 'Abbeygate Apartments'. With all mod cons such as central heating and private parking, it was part of the conservation area stipulations that any modernisation such as double glazing to muffle the sounds from the High Street would have to be carried out sympathetically to the original Neo Georgian style windows, this has been achieved admirably which is aesthetically pleasing to the eye.

It's Summer 1936 when these photographs were taken of Wavertree Gardens from the High Street, within the square and from the 'Mystery'.

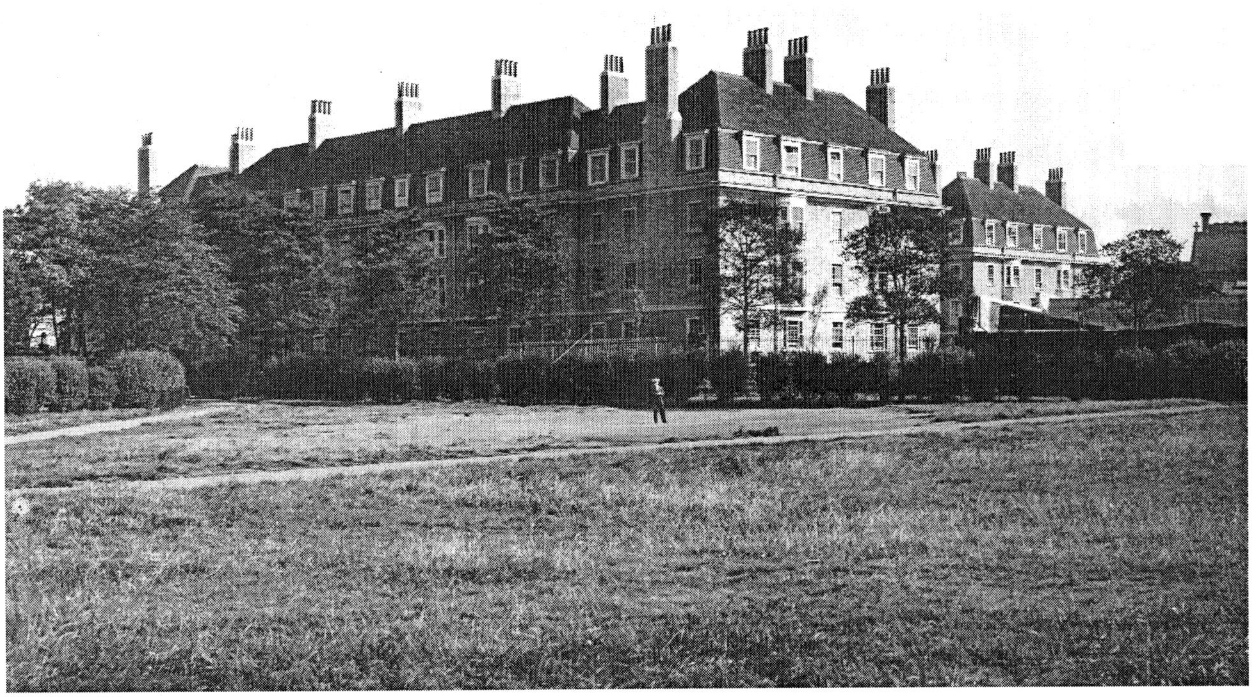

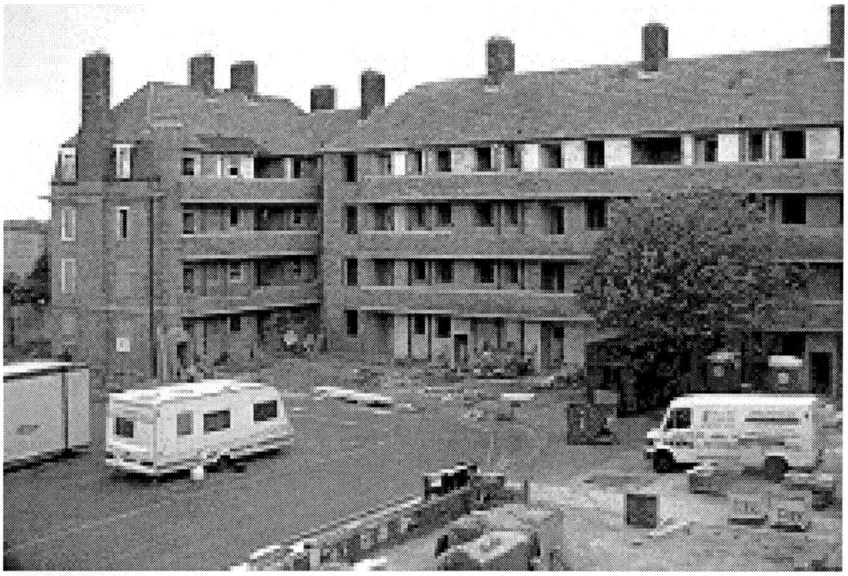

Wavertree Gardens during its renovation and part of the redeveloped complex from the new security gates.

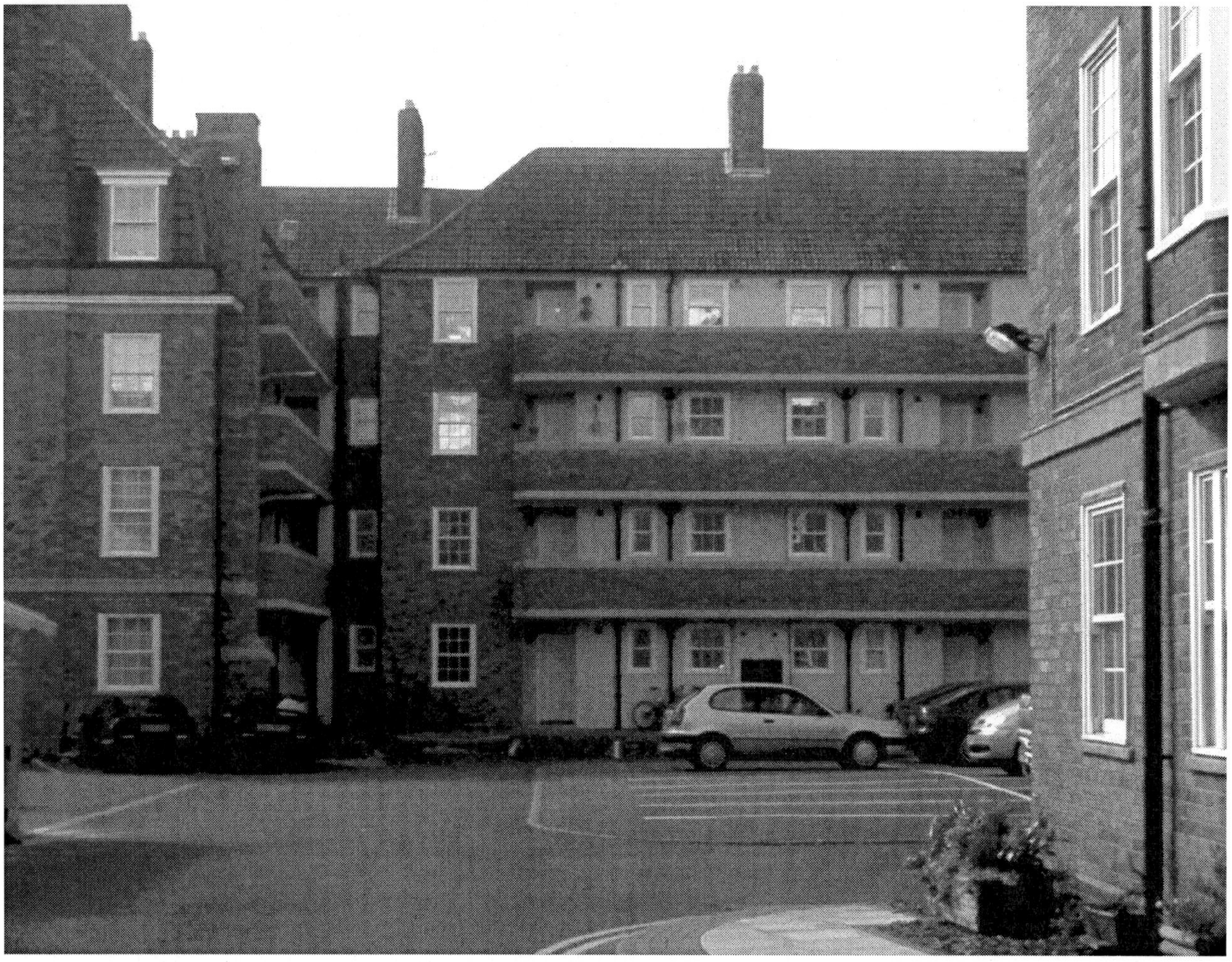

TUEBROOK

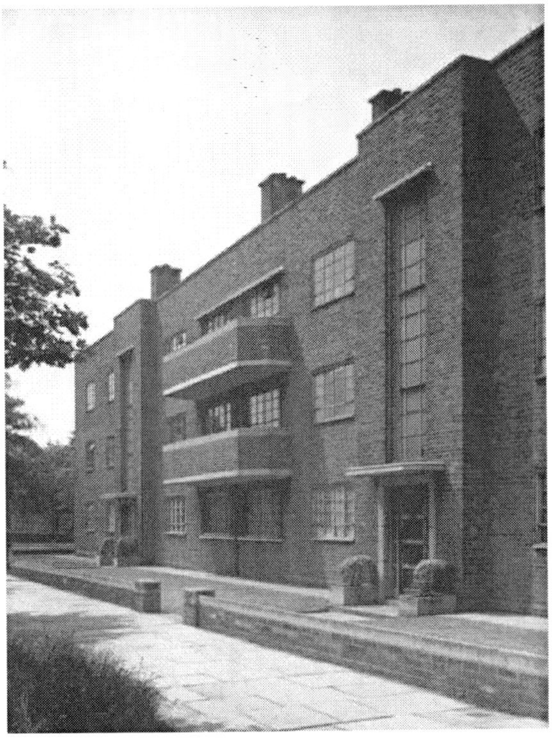

Muirhead Avenue, the main thoroughfare leading to Norris Green, another of Lancelot Keay's townships, houses a small block of tenements on the Green Lane roundabout which also extend onto West Derby Road. Originally modelled as the Larkhill Estate flats for single persons, they were sold to the Regenda Group in 2006 for renovation into 21 two and, strangely, just 1 three bedroom apartments for sale.

Higher up Muirhead Avenue on the opposite, north side just before Queens Drive, a few blocks still exist, one of which backs onto Adshead Road in the Clubmoor district. With wood cladded back verandas and just three storeys high, like all the property in this area, these blocks now

A 1944 and a 2006 view of the Larkhill Estate flats on West Derby Road, Tuebrook.

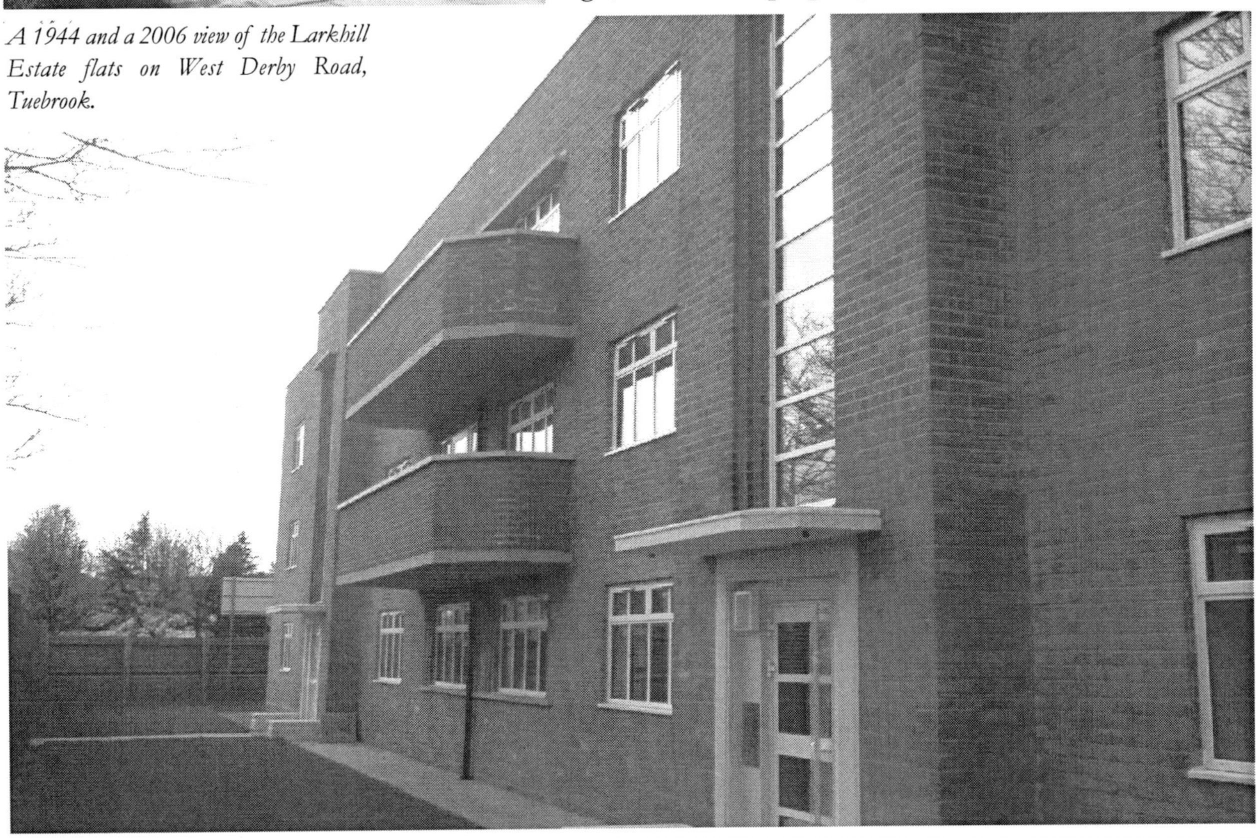

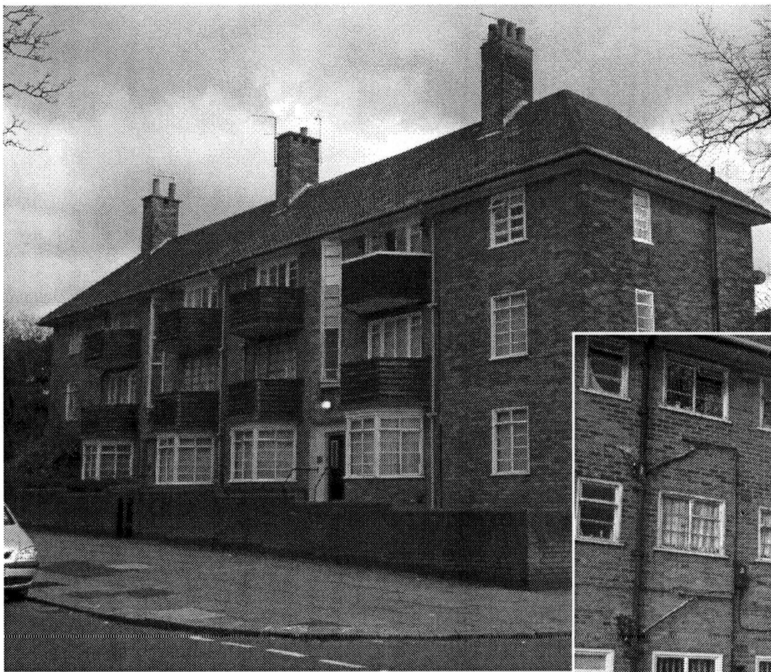

contain a security door entrance. Although grand looking from the main road, the front side landings which house just a single flat either side of the stairwell and the cabbage patch central garden look tired, dated and in need of a little TLC from the City Council.

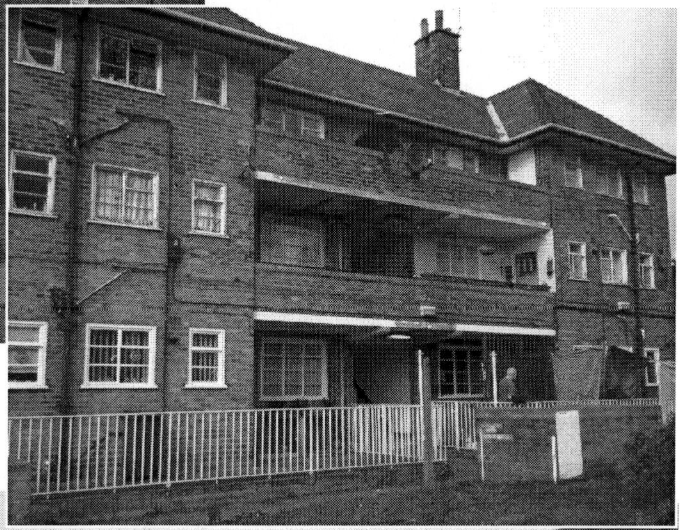

A front and back view of the flats bounded by Muirhead Avenue, Adshead Road and Ballantyne Road, Clubmoor.

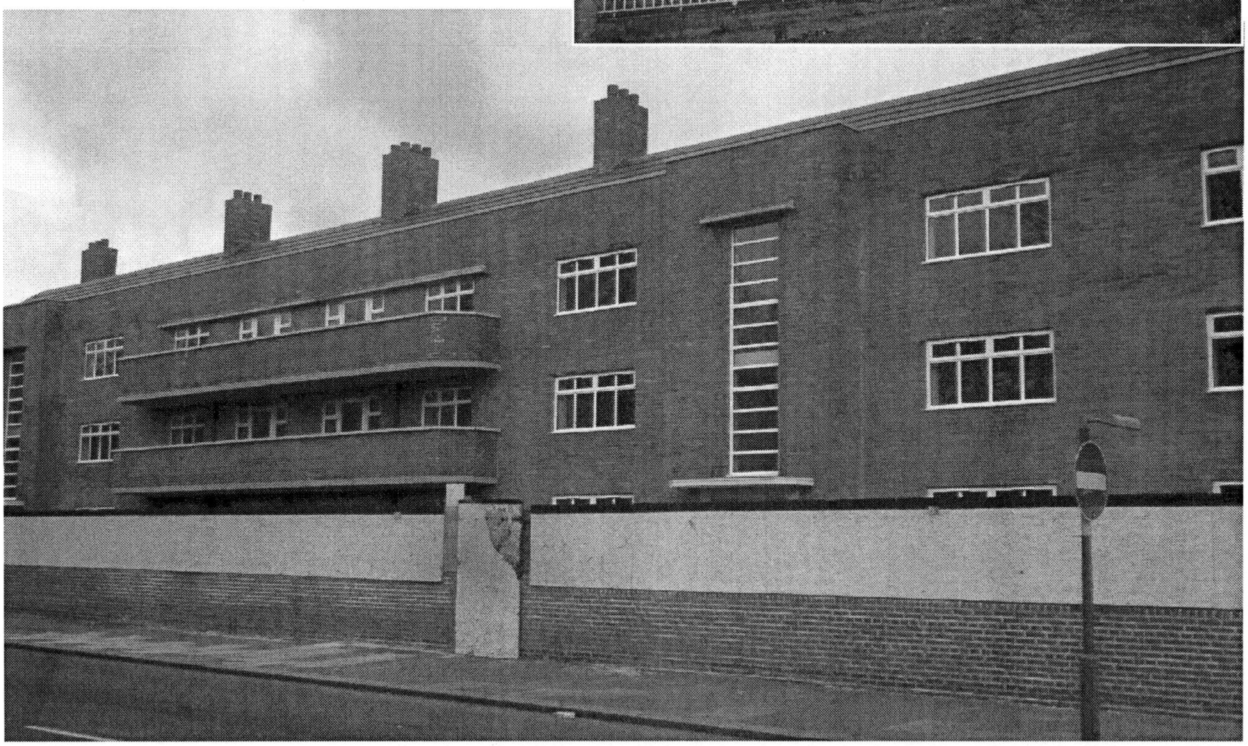

OLD SWAN

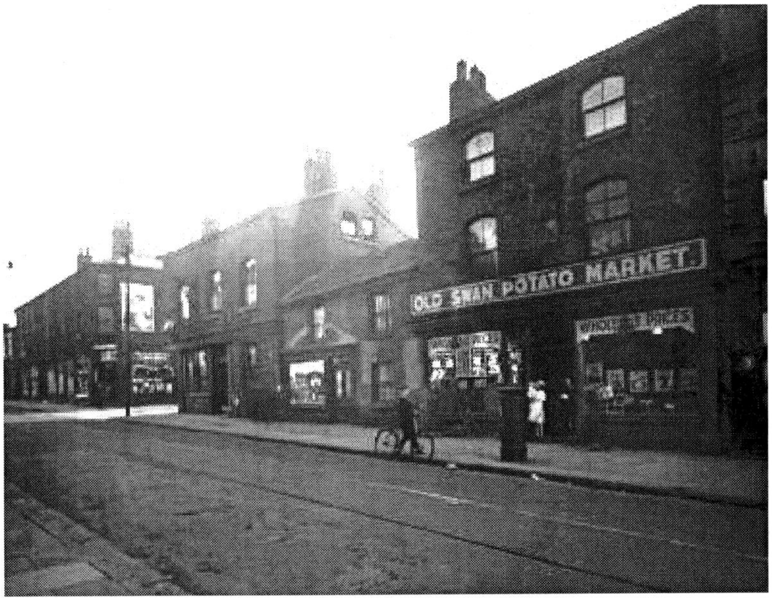

1937 and Old Swan Potato Market, The Royal Standard Public House, Rock House and Richard Williams Engineering Works were all under Compulsory Purchase Orders from local arbitrators and Chartered Surveyors, Francis J. Kirby so that owners could be compensated to allow for the demolition of their premises. St. Oswald Street was then widened and St. Oswald's House and Gardens tenements were built.

Located to the East of Fairfield and Stanley and to the north of Wavertree, Liverpool 13 was home to a number of inter war tenement developments built between 1938 and 1939. Edwardian Old Swan would have seen a rope walks and reservoir on the west Side of St. Oswald's Street before the Elms House Estate was laid out. Hoult's corner on the junction of St. Oswald's Street and Prescot Road was partly cleared to make way for St. Oswald's House, a newly created curved development of tenement flats which housed a row of shops beneath. The remainder of the old property which existed at the old junction was then demolished leaving an uninterrupted view of the new flats. Rock Street, which ran at the back of this development housed St. Oswald's Gardens.

At the south end of St. Oswald's Street at its junction with Edge Lane Drive, a further complex was constructed. Hurst Gardens were situated on the prominent tram and bus route to and from the city centre and indeed, some years later, the M62 approach road. Originally Springfield Street until its junction with Mill Lane, Edge Lane Drive is therefore now busier than ever, being the continuation of Edge Lane which is so called as it's the ancient boundary positioned along the edge of the township of West Derby which divides it from

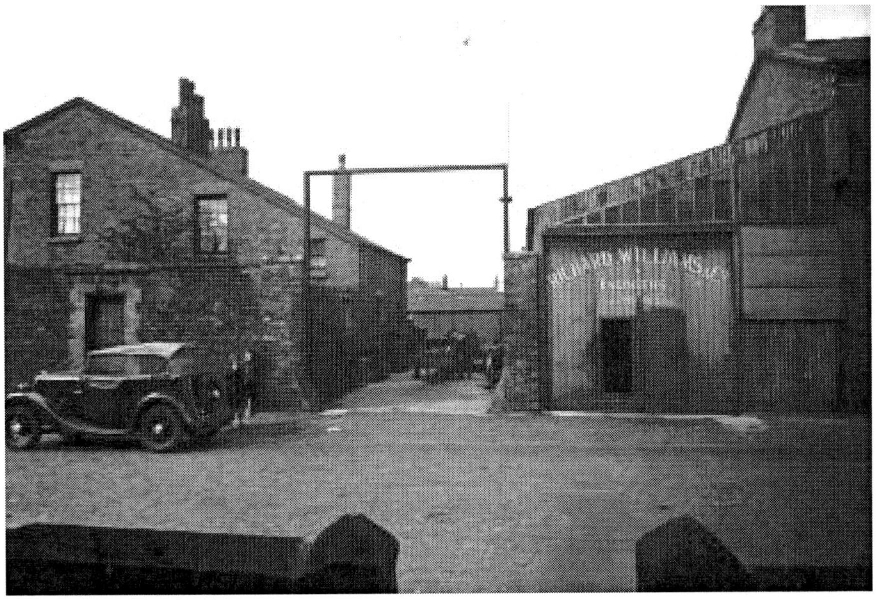

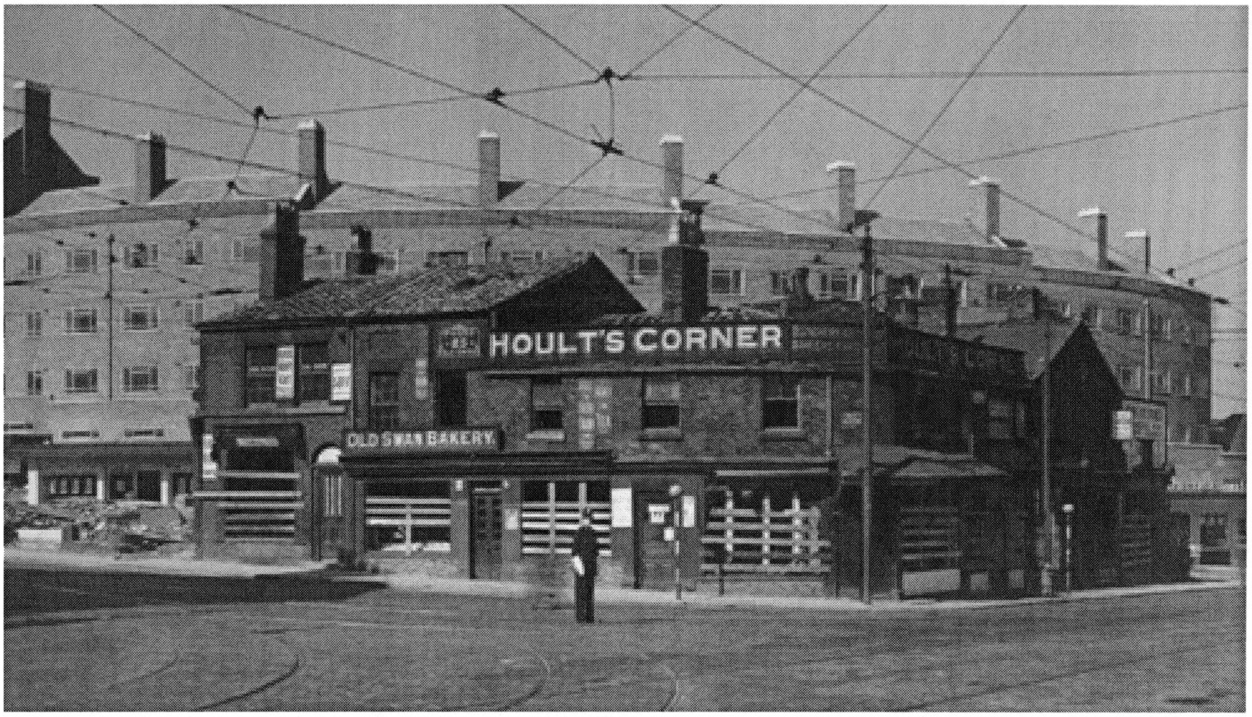

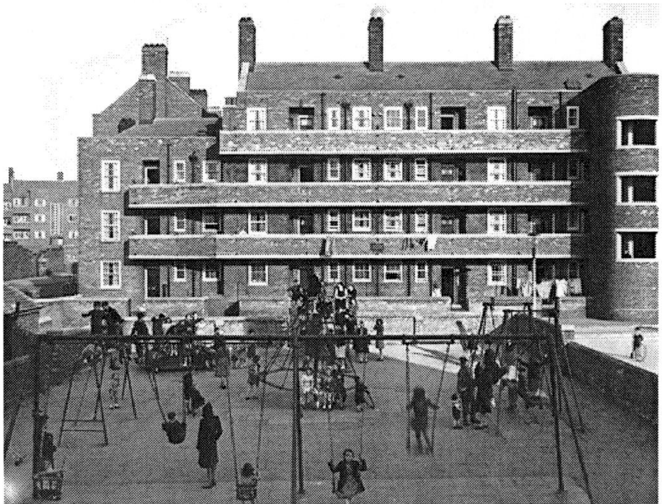

St. Oswald's House had been built behind these old shops on Hoult's corner in 1939. Upon demolition of the old shops a few weeks later, the new tenements and shops are ready for occupation. A Tesco supermarket now stands on this site

neighbouring Wavertree. The Queens Arms public house which separated the Hurst Gardens tenement blocks was demolished in 1957 and rebuilt as the Paraffin Oil Shop public house which is still open for business today.

The playground and tenement block belonging to St. Oswald's Gardens, Old Swan.

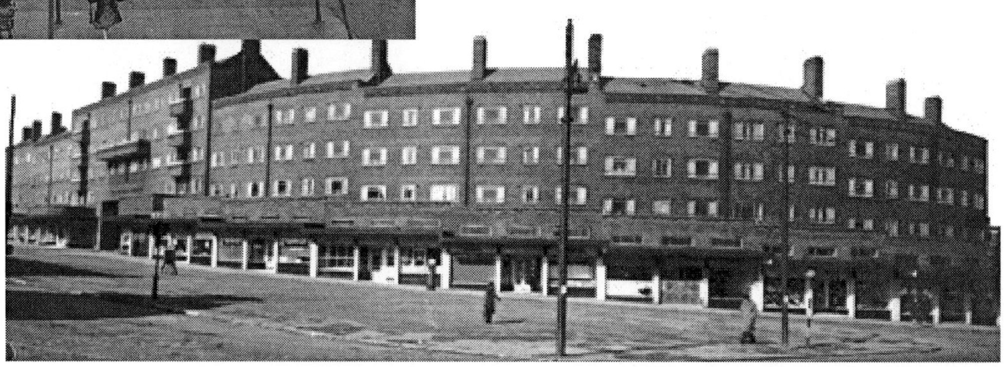

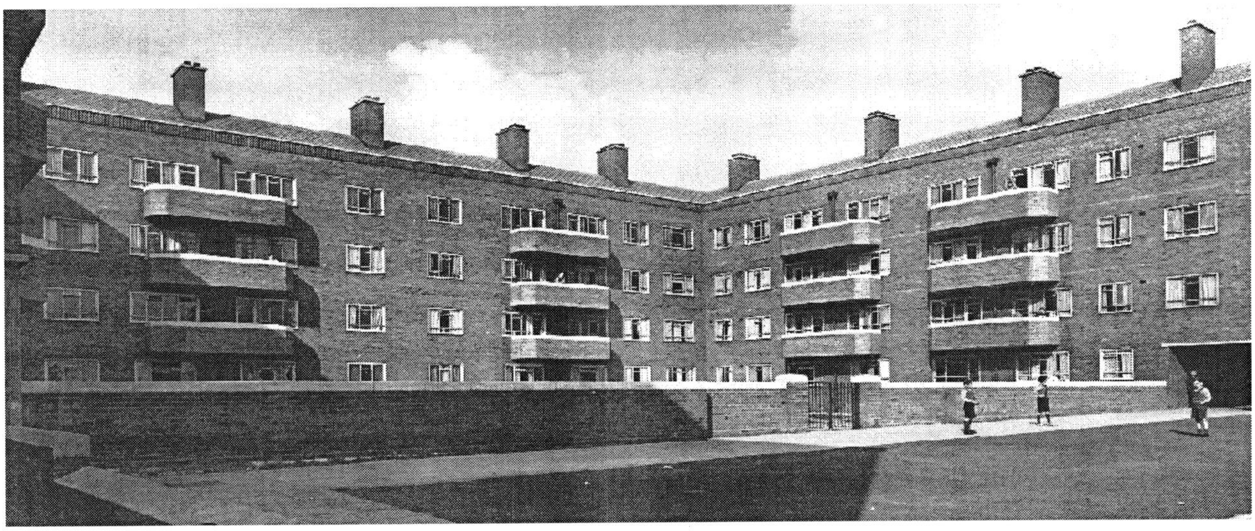

Hurst Gardens located on Hurst Street off Edge Lane Drive - 1948

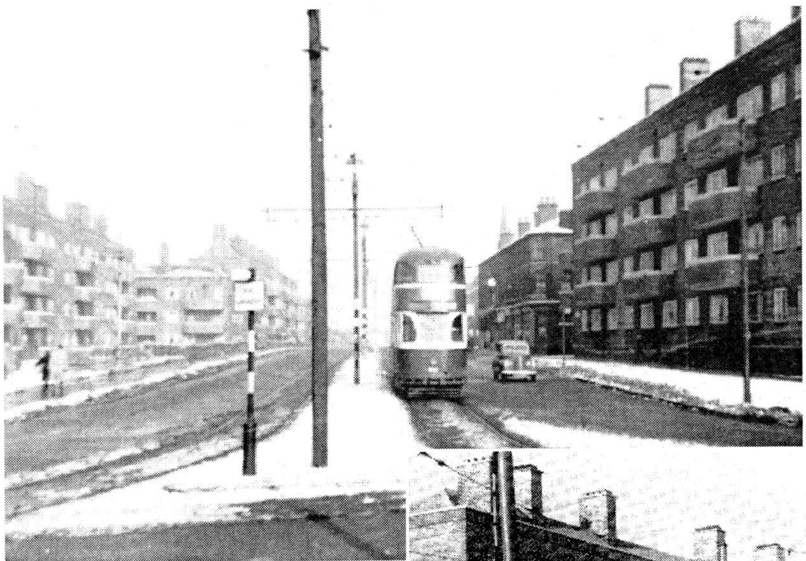

The last week of service of car No. 992 on peak hour route 41 Page Moss to Edge Lane. St. Oswald's Gardens are on the left, Hurst Gardens are on the right.

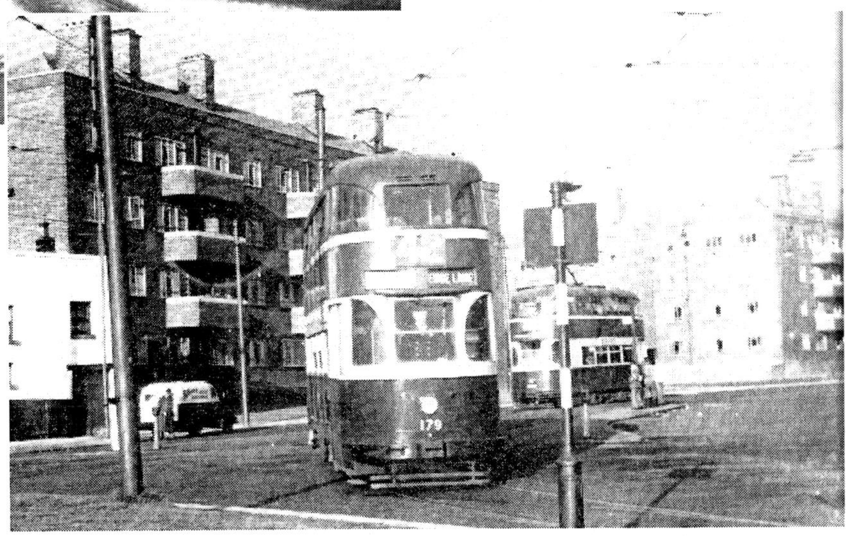

Hurst Gardens is the backdrop in this photograph featuring baby grand car 272 on the 49 route to Penny Lane and car 179 nearing its terminus at Edge Lane.

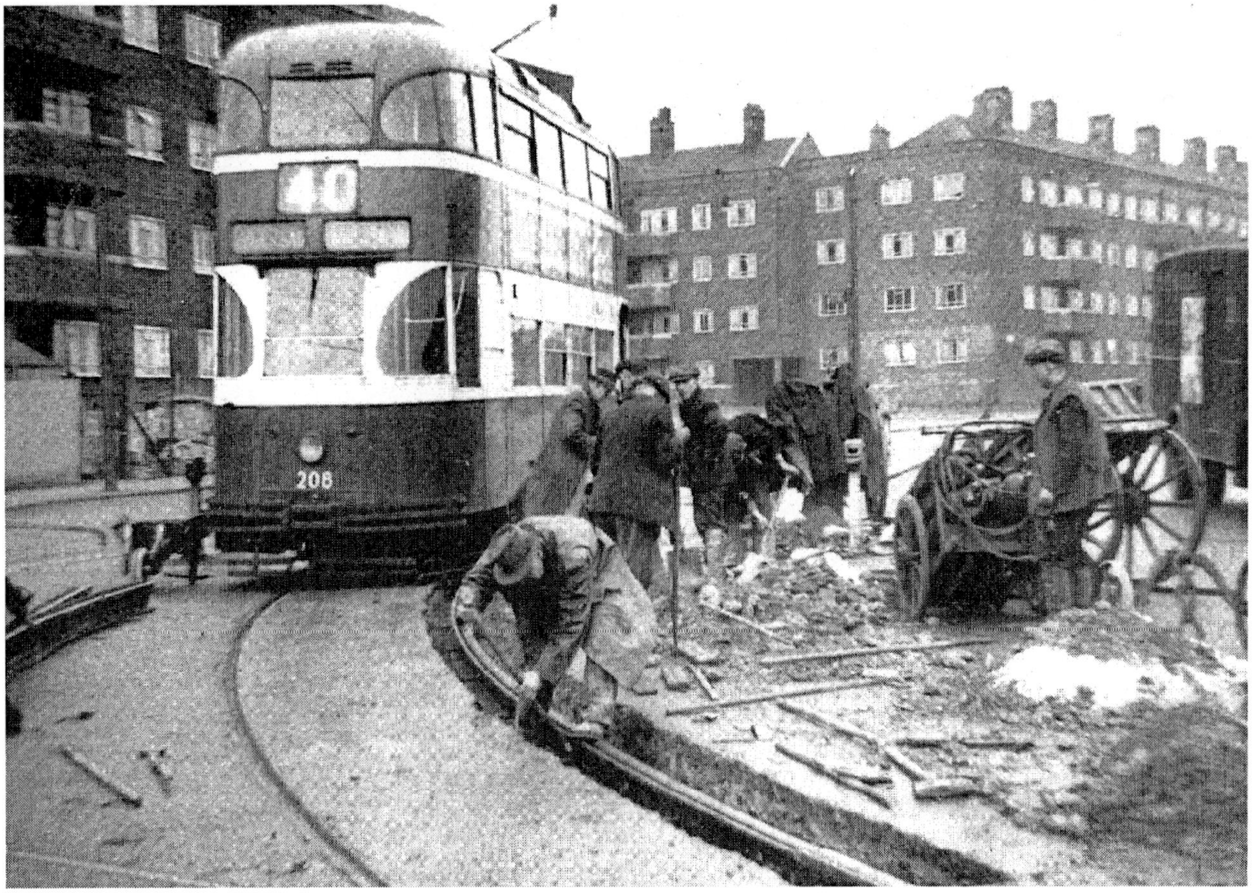

The No.40 is going nowhere fast as a track gang repair some worn curves on the Edge Lane roundabout in the winter of 1956. Hurst Gardens again features.

Hurst Gardens is divided by the old Queens Arms Public House, rebuilt in 1957 and still trading today as the Paraffin Oil Shop. The mansion on the right was later demolished to make way for the new road layout, yet another act of wanton vandalism.

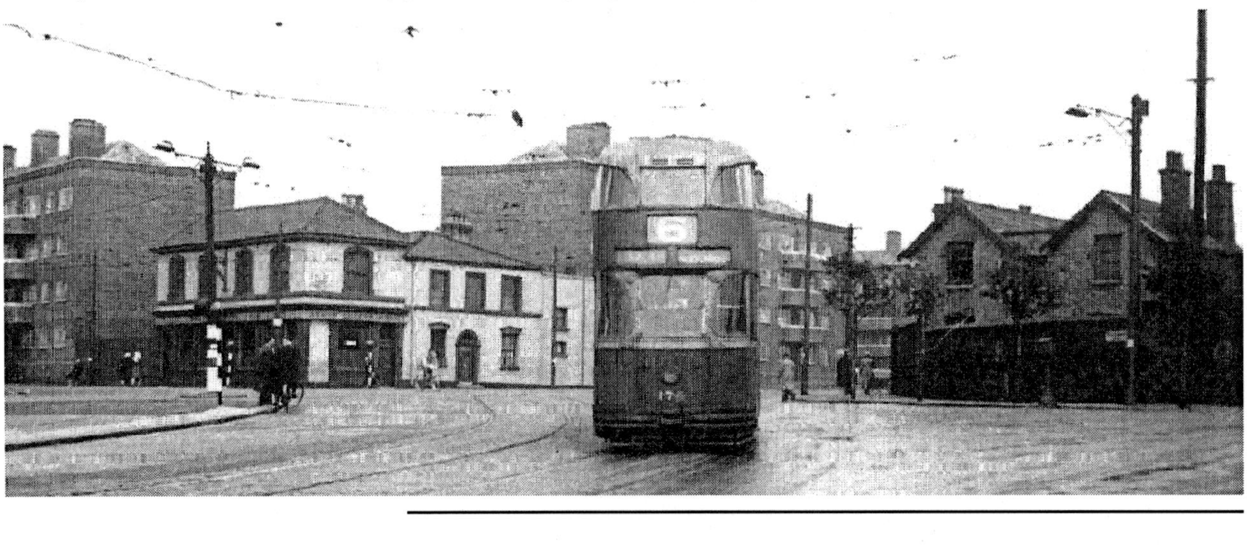

Blackhorse Lane flats in Old Swan. A small corner block built on a diagonal which looks every bit as 1930s as ever apart from the car and the wheelie bins in the small square. It's quite an oddity that it should remain when grander schemes bit the dust, but thankful of its 21st century existence all the same. The outer view is from East Prescot Road.

A very small block of flats are still situated on the corner of East Prescot Road and Black Horse Lane, L13. Only three storeys high and devoid of the usual back veranda's, the main archway to the small square which fronts onto the back gardens of neighbouring houses is on a block that runs diagonally between the two aforementioned streets. This arch now contains the type of security door to the stairwell that has been added to the 1950s standard unit blocks of flats and maisonettes.

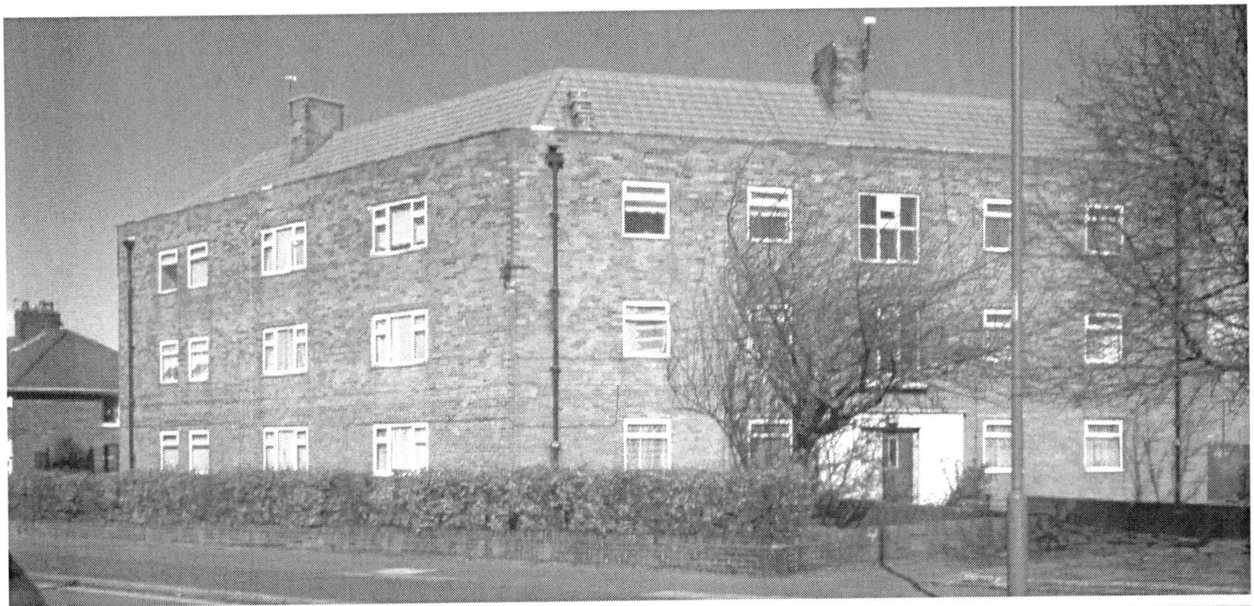

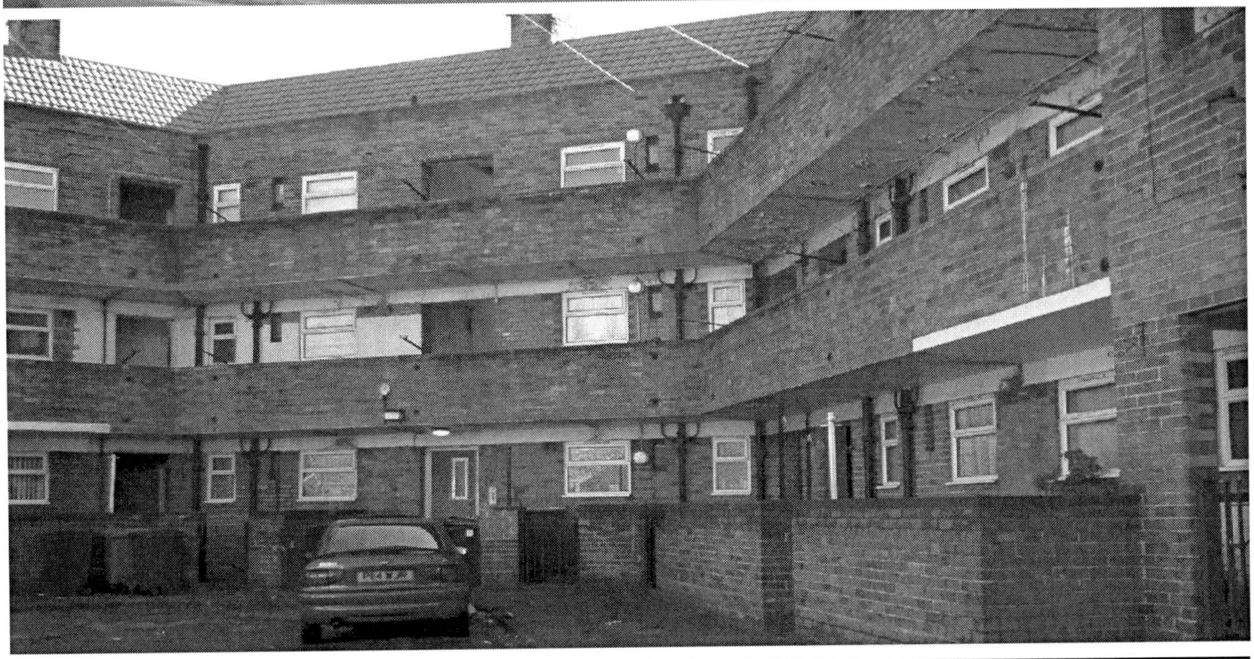

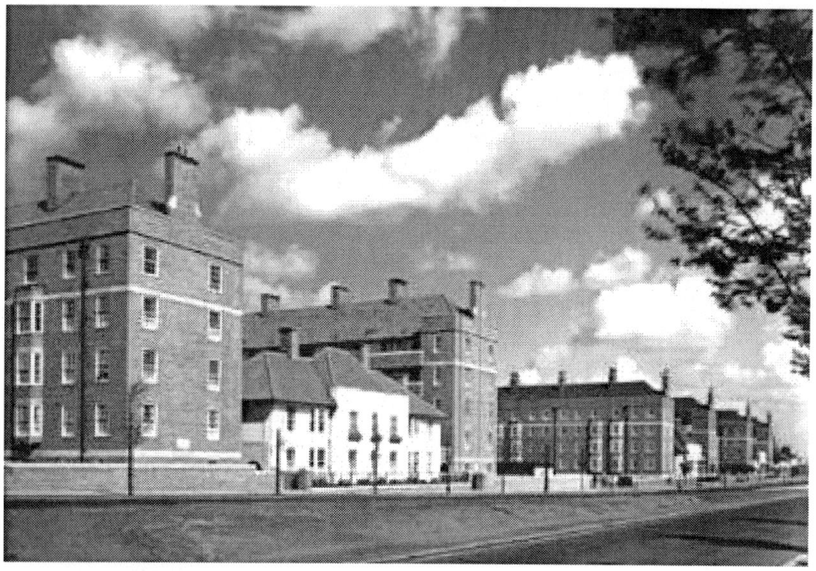

Speke Road Gardens as newly constructed in 1937.

THE SOUTH END

SPEKE AND GARSTON

Speke Road Gardens were built in 1932 on the East side of Speke Road, the main artery from Garston to Speke which was laid out in 1921. These tenements stood facing Banks Road and were situated not far from the Speke Freight Terminal railway sidings.

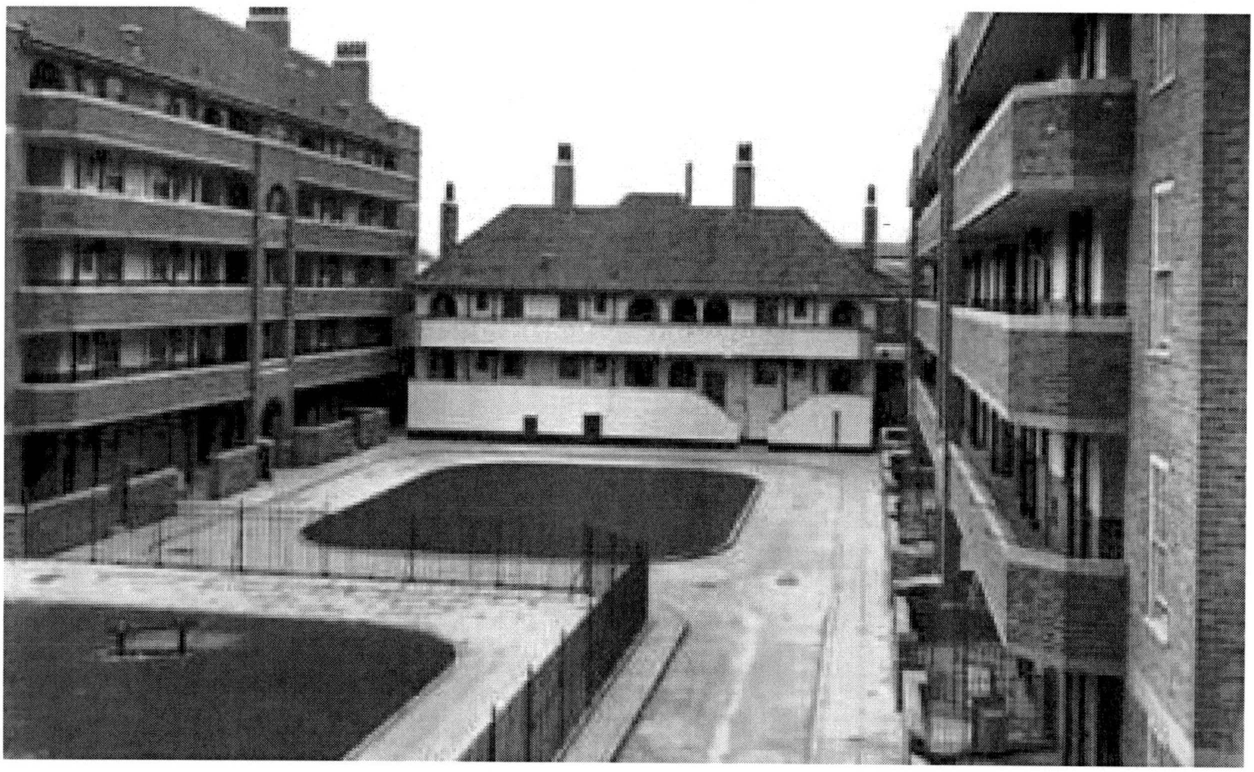

The land was previously that of Cowen's nursery gardens but before that it was once the vineyard of the world famous Mr. Meredith whose grapes were noted as second to none. Vineyard Street and Meredith

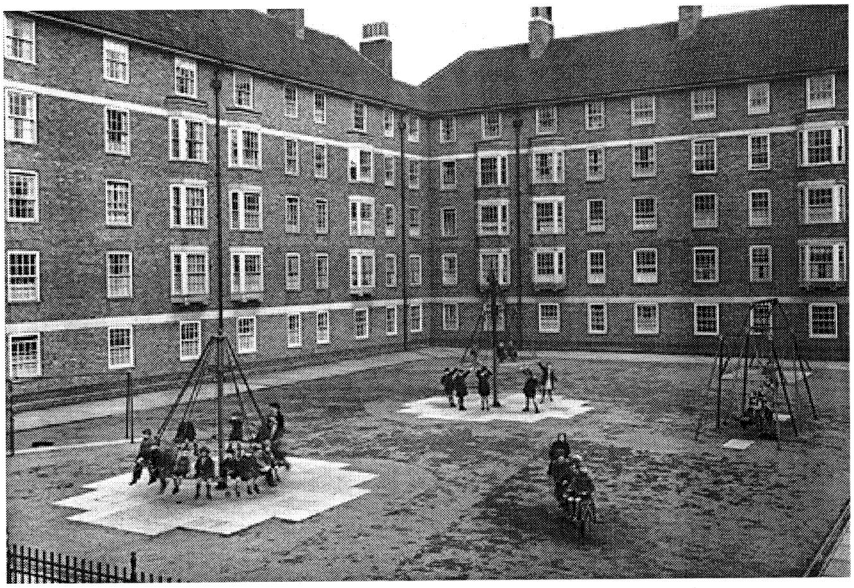

Speke Road Gardens as newly constructed in 1937.

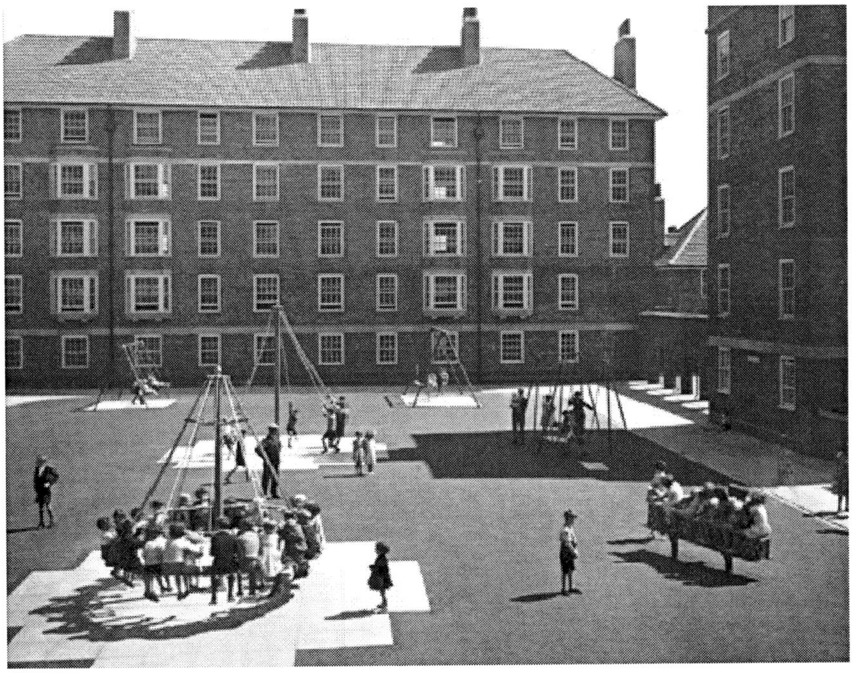

Street which ran to the rear of the tenements were in fact laid out in his honour. The flats themselves were demolished in 1983.

Speke newtown was one of Lancelot Keay's most notable achievements. As an award winning scheme, the Speke Township became a model for self contained municipal housing estates throughout the world.

Speke Township was created from scratch in the 1930s under the directive of Lancelot Keay, Liverpool's chief housing architect. Built between Speke Boulevard which is the main artery to Widnes and Runcorn, and Hale Road which leads to Hale Village, evidence still exists at the East end of Western Avenue where flats were built in a similar style to those in Muirhead avenue but without landings. However they do feature a windowed stairway with the art deco trademark arch in Tarbock Road. At the West (airport) end of Western Avenue, flats were built over a row of shops, again an arch features in Damwood Road.

Central Avenue, which together with Central Way, links Western and Eastern Avenue contained similar flats in a curve at Conleach Road and Ganworth Road but these have now been replaced with modern apartments.

DINGLE AND TOXTETH

Dingle Mount is seen here on the bend into Dingle Lane whilst South Hill House is on the left beyond Balkan Street. The year is 1969.

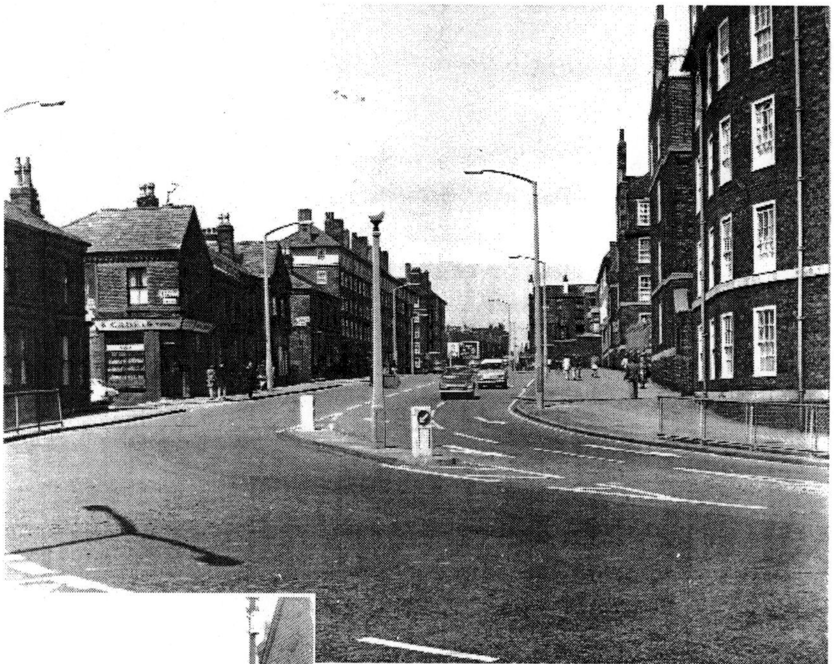

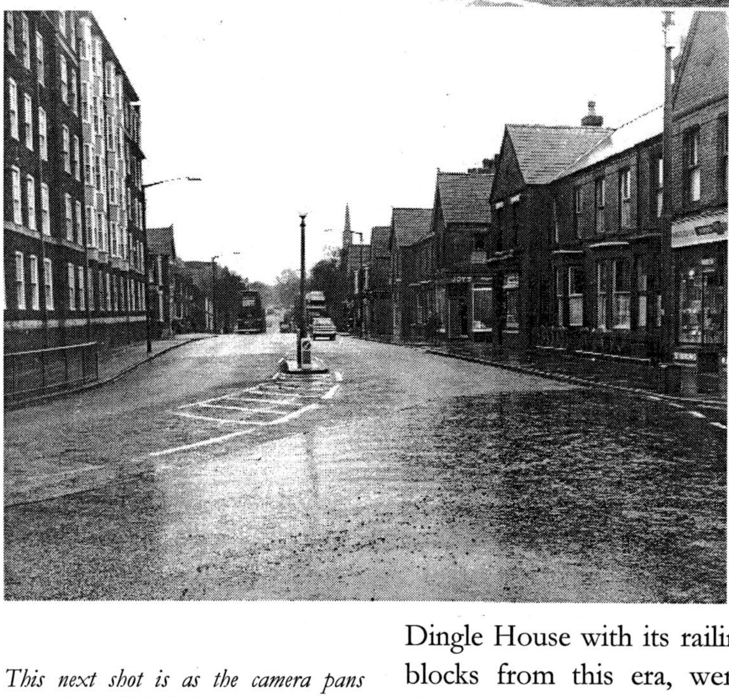

The Dingle area stretches primarily from Dingle Lane in the south to Parliament Street in the north and to the West side and just East of Park Road. This includes the once thriving south docks complex which consisted of Herculaneum, Toxteth and Brunswick docks. The land has since been reclaimed for new build apartments, hotels, restaurants and prestige car showrooms. The block bounded by Dingle Lane, Dingle Mount and south Hill Road was home to a number of tenements.

This next shot is as the camera pans around into Dingle Lane as seen from Dingle Vale.

Dingle House with its railing landings were from 1923. A feature of blocks from this era, were that nearly all of the recessed front doorstep entrances to the top landing contained an archway.

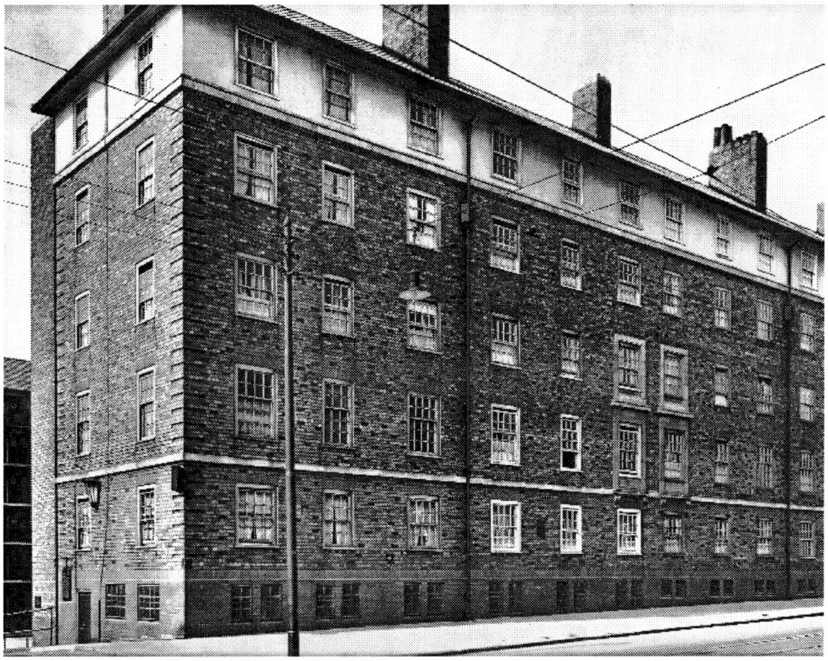

Somehow, when nearing the end of their lifespan in the mid 1980s, these older blocks looked a bit tattier than those from a decade later which contained the walled landings.

Nearby, Dingle Mount was on the thoroughfare of the same name which was the southern continuation of Beloe Street and rounded the corner into Dingle Lane itself. South Hill House built in 1932 contained a sunken central garden in its 'backie', created due to its location below street level and accessed by a flight of steps. This gave allowance for an extra sixth storey of flats. South Hill Road was so called because it was laid out across the South Hill at Dingle Boundary with the old Toxteth Park Estate. The tenements previously described were built on the site of many institutions that existed in the area.

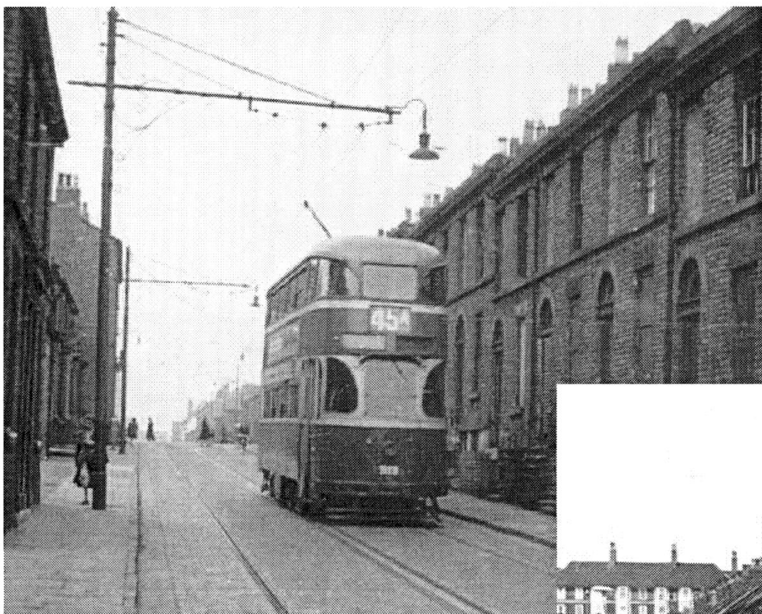

The last service of the 45A tram proceeding down Beloe Street in September 1951. The close proximity of the tram lines on this street means that the trams couldn't pass each other here.

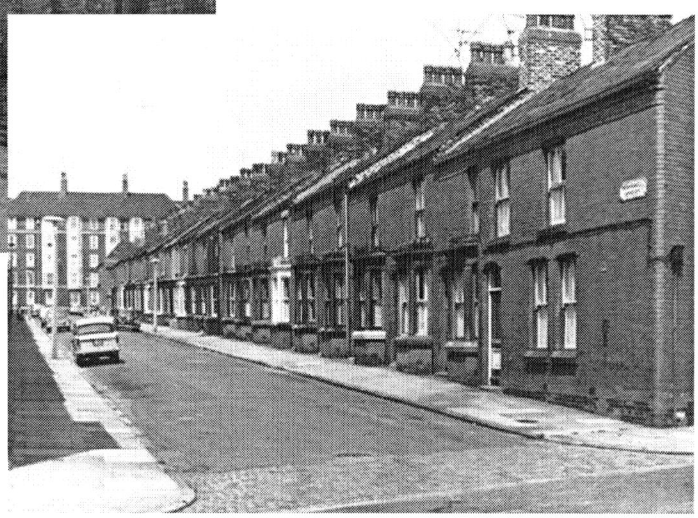

Monkswell Street in 1969, the picture was taken from Hind Street looking towards Dingle Lane.

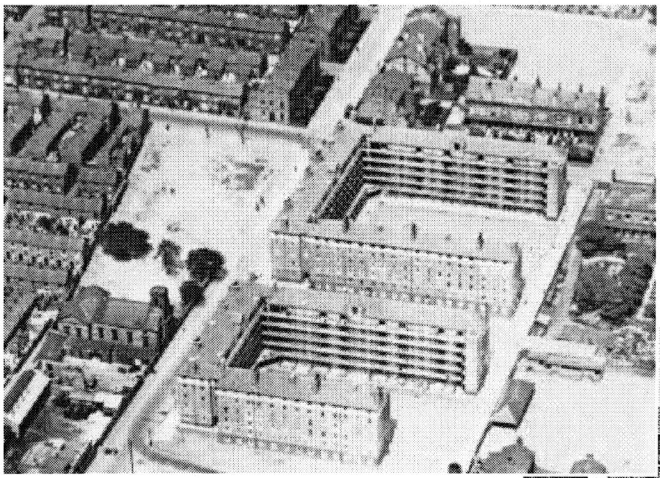

1947 and an aerial view of South Hill Road and Dingle Road showing the tenements.

Part of the female paupers hospital as well as the girls industrial school, the benevolent institution and South Hill Vicarage were all cleared in the late 1920s along with a number of themed streets.

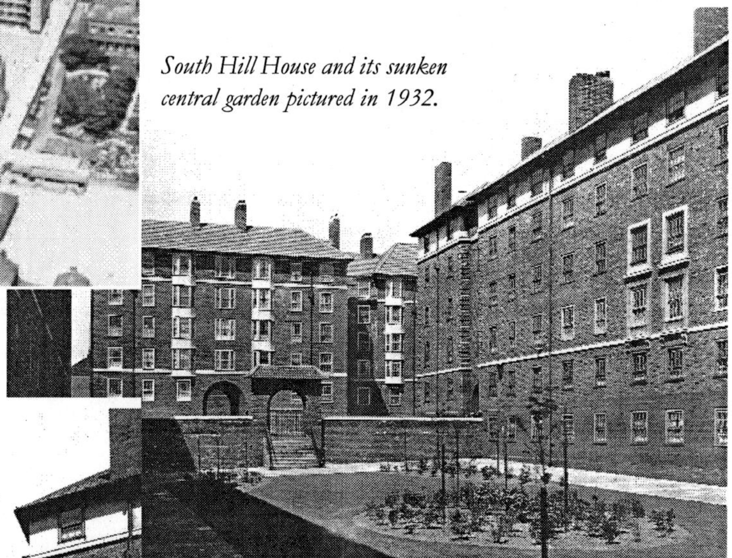

South Hill House and its sunken central garden pictured in 1932.

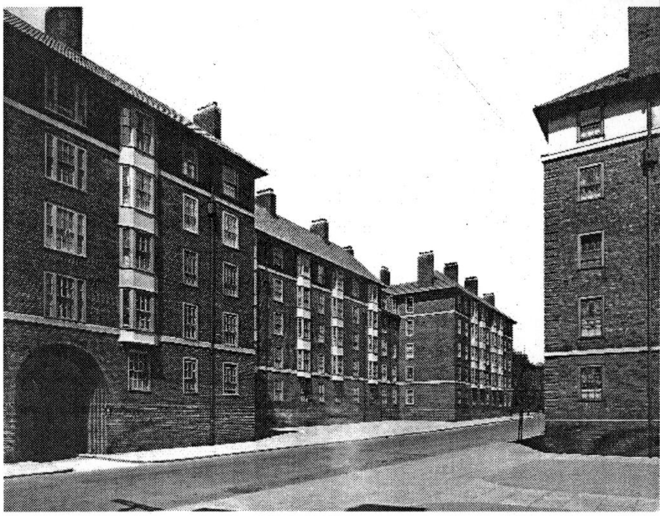

South Hill Road, showing the flats looking towards Beloe Street in 1932.

These were Emerald and Ruby Street to the north of South Hill Road and Bosnia, Plevna and Balkan Street to the south. Beloe Street which ran across south Hill Road from Mill Street to Dingle Mount was named in commemoration of Charles Henry Beloe, a

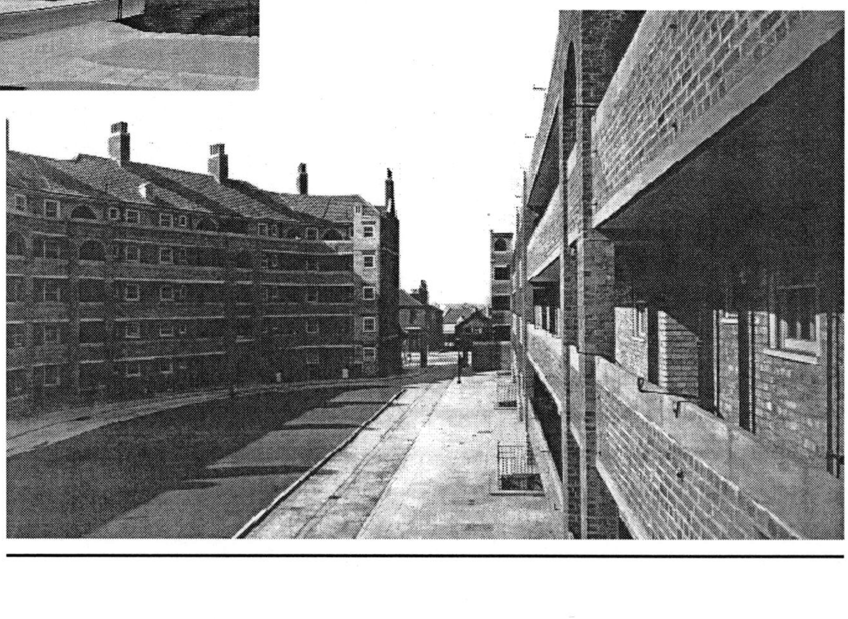

Dingle Mount Square - 1932

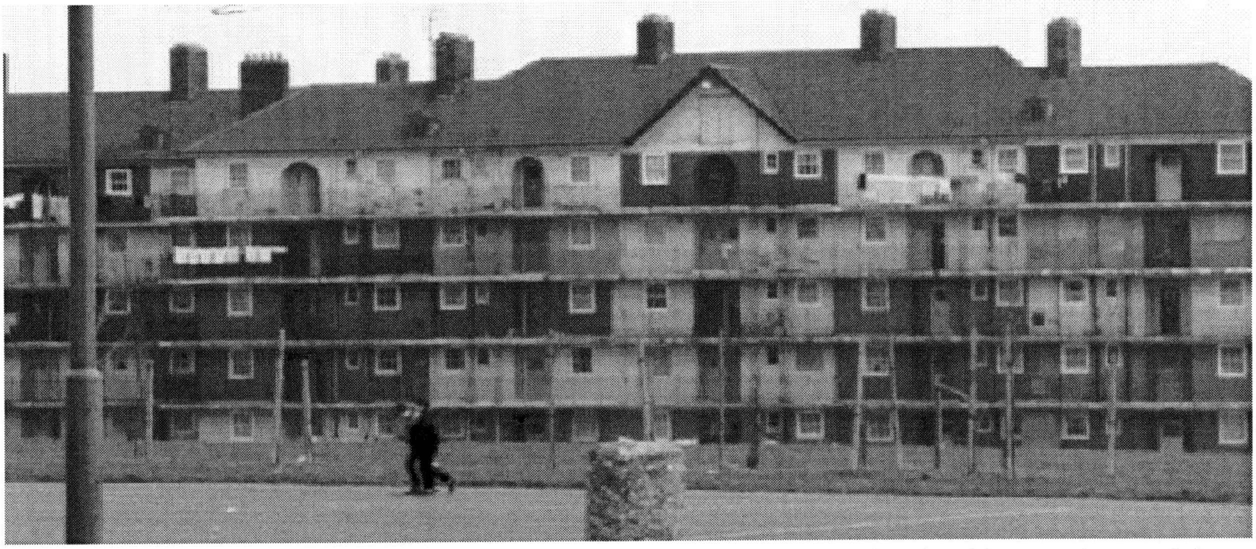

Fronted by a tarmac football pitch, these blocks in Dingle hailed from the 1920s.

civil engineer and Liberal Councillor for the Abercromby ward from 1892 to 1902.

Rankin Street, sandwiched between Beresford Road and Wellington Road housed a tenement block which was very similar in design to that in Great Richmond Street, Liverpool 3. Hailing from the late 1920s, these were three and four storey blocks with the traditional railing landings and arched top landing doorway, built to replace the slum terracing and courts that previously existed there. Rankin Street itself was abolished in the late 1990s when the area was revamped with new housing.

Grafton Street, named after the 18th Century Whig PM, Lord Grafton, runs the full length of Dingle from Parliament Street to Dingle Lane. It was here that Grafton House, one of a number of tenement blocks stood until the 1980s. Lower down, towards the docks is Caryl Street. This was named after Caryl, the 3rd Viscount Molyneux who were the owners of the vast majority of Toxteth Park. Lord Street in the city centre is also named in commemoration of him.

Rankin Street flats off Beresford Road.

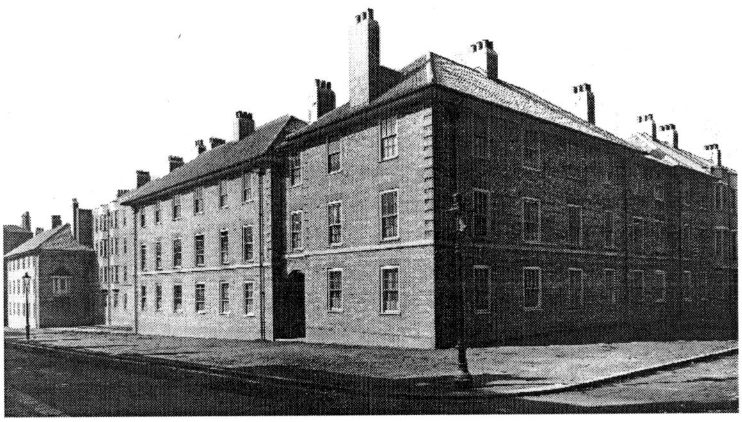

Between Northumberland Street and Park Street stood Brunswick Gardens. These occupied the full block facing the

Brunswick Goods depot which served cargo entering neighbouring Brunswick and Toxteth docks. Built symmetrically, its central archway was situated in the longer middle block which was set back from the main street of Caryl Street and its accompanying blocks at either end. Constructed between 1936 and 1938 as part of a large scale five storey development along with Warwick Gardens and Caryl Gardens, these blocks mainly replaced old saw mills and timber yards and as such, there was not much demolition involved.

Heading north towards the city centre and across Northumberland Street, the south annex to the new Liverpool hospital on Hill Street stood. Having served the south end community for over 100 years it was closed and demolished in the 1970s. Sharing the same block, were a saw mill, timber yard and St. Thomas-in-the-fields Church dating from 1841 which stood on the corner of Warwick Street and Grafton Street. These were demolished in 1935 to make way for Warwick Gardens.

Facing these tenements across Warwick Street stood Caryl Gardens which took up the whole block to Hill Street. Again, storage yards were cleared and Back Grafton Street, a court infested dead end was abolished. Caryl Gardens were another impressive symmetrical development and in keeping with the other tenements springing up in the city, no two complexes were alike. The vast monotony of block upon block of brick was broken up by introducing a white stucco finish to the corners of the blocks of Caryl and Grafton Street and to the whole blocks which were accessed from Hill Street and Warwick Street. As with Brunswick Gardens, the main arched entrance was set back from Caryl Street with landscaped gardens and ornamental lighting to either side.

This Northumberland Street terrace was still going strong when pictured here in 1960.

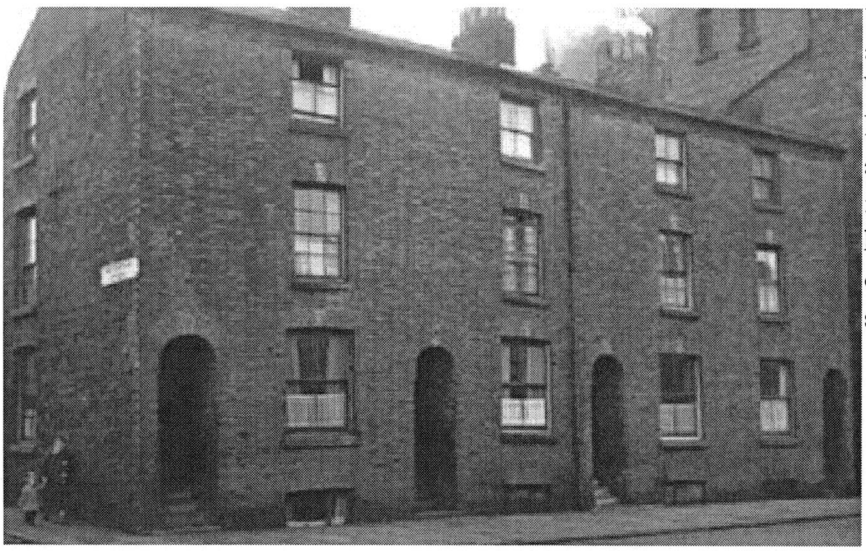

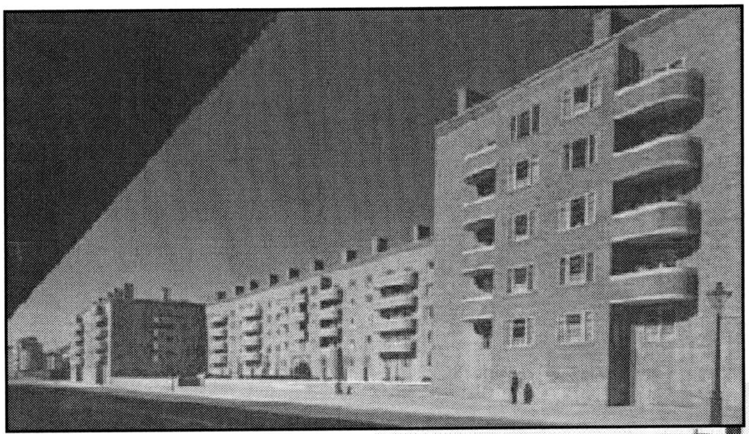

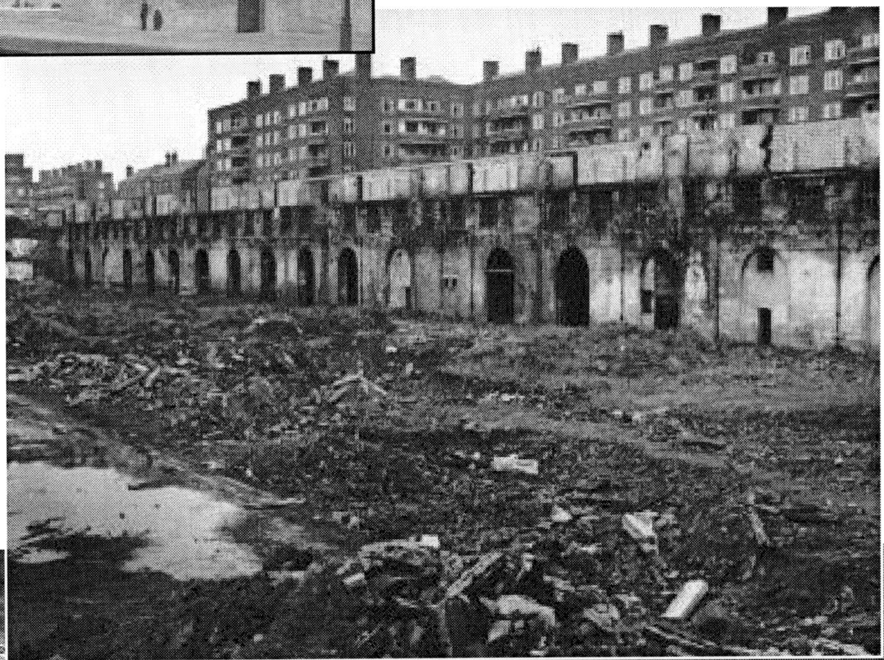

Brunswick Gardens stood majestically above the dock landfill site immediately opposite to the goods sheds. Another view, both to the north and to the south along Caryl Street was taken in 1938.

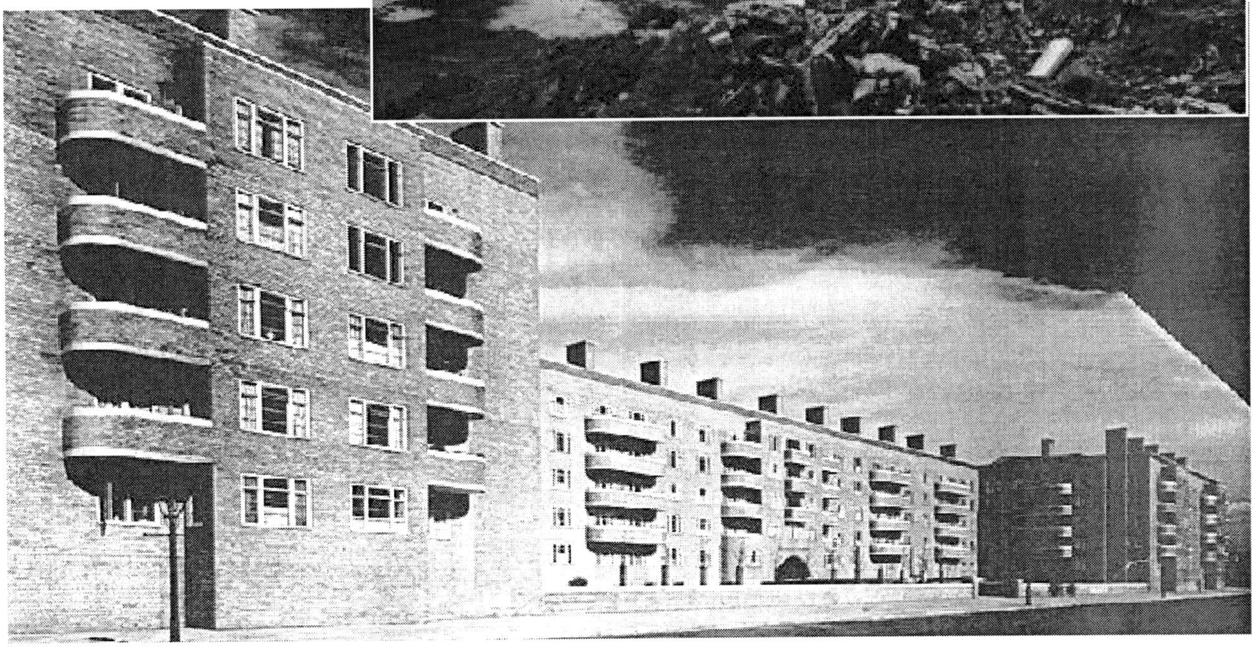

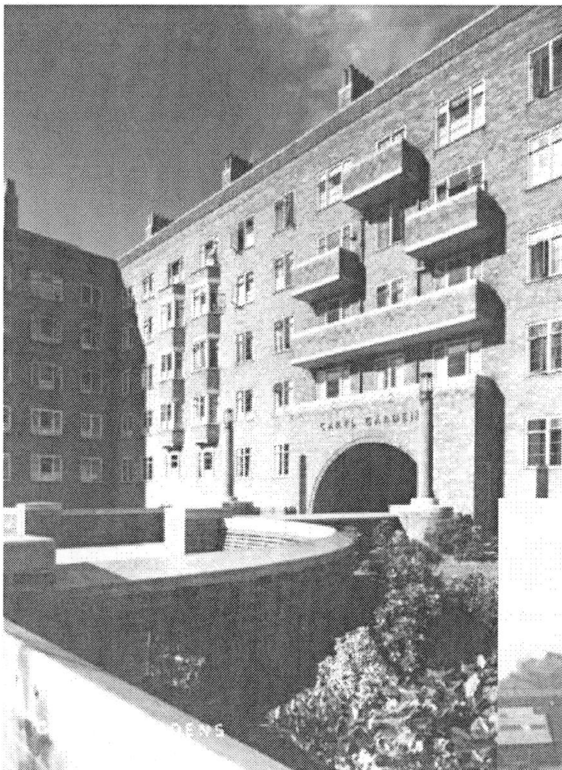

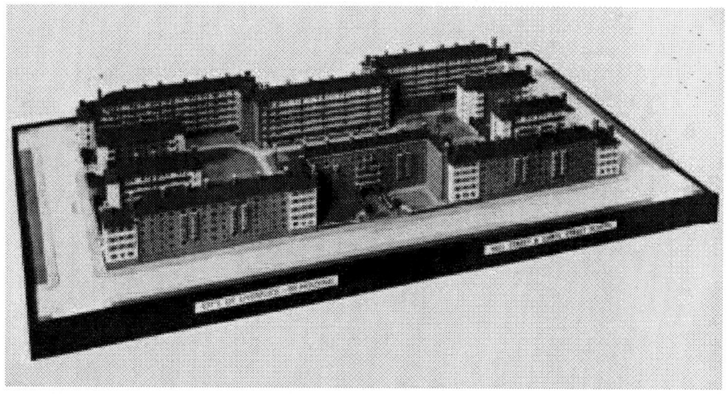

A model of Caryl Gardens created by Liverpool Corporation designers Robson & Marsden viewed here in 1935 clearly shows the symmetrical formation of the blocks from above.

With sweeping curved walls, well proportioned gardens and ornamental lighting, Caryl Gardens in 1938 would offer hundreds of new flats to the locals of Dingle

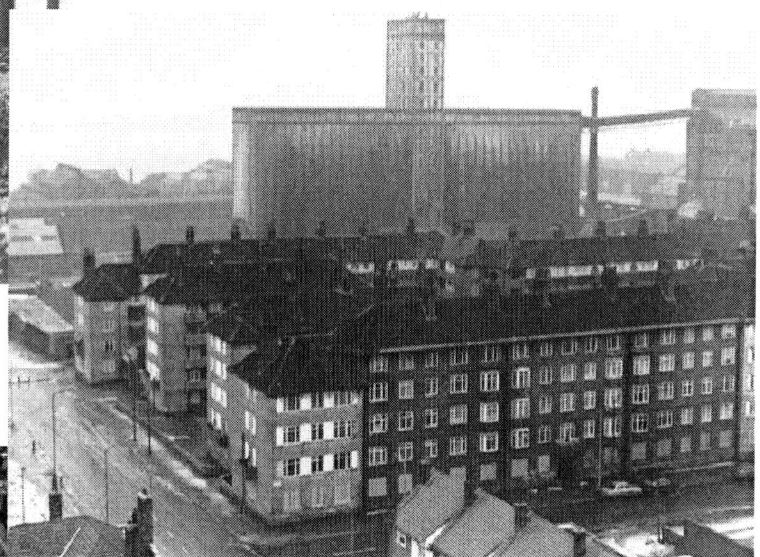

Taken from Sandside View high rise on Warwick Street. Caryl Gardens are seen here on the junction of Grafton Street and Warwick Street. The large Wilson King mill was on Brunswick Dock

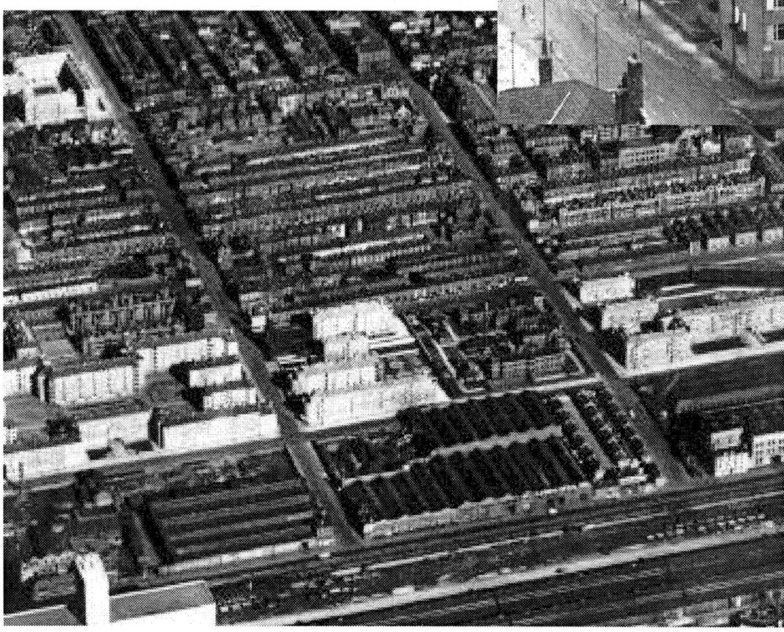

A view of Brunswick Dock showing the close proximity of Sussex, Caryl, Warwick and Brunswick Gardens on Dingle's landscape.

Warwick Street at its junction with Park Road becomes Upper Warwick Street. To the rear of the Royal Oak Public House which still stands on this junction, were Sussex Gardens. Sussex Street which ran from Upper Warwick Street to Upper Hill Street had eleven court ridden streets that ran off it, the last of which were flattened by the mid 1940s which was relatively late compared to others. South Chester Street, Back South Chester Street, Rockbrook Street, Coburg Street, Luke Street, Jenner Street, Spring Street, Bryan Street, Lansdowne Street, Devonshire Street and Southampton Street were replaced with these four and five storey tenements.

Built in 1950, these were to be the last blocks built in the city of the inter-war, walk up landing flats design as by now the city council were introducing lifts to all previously built blocks that exceeded three storeys or a landing length of more than six flats. Constructed to accommodate the post war housing shortage, the council's policy changed in that same year to the building of smaller three storey blocks in a standard unit. These contained an internal, enclosed staircase and landing accessed via a main 'square arch' entrance. Many of these flats still exist in parts of Liverpool today having been updated to include a security door with intercom system and some have even had the top floor demolished so that they could be adapted into houses.

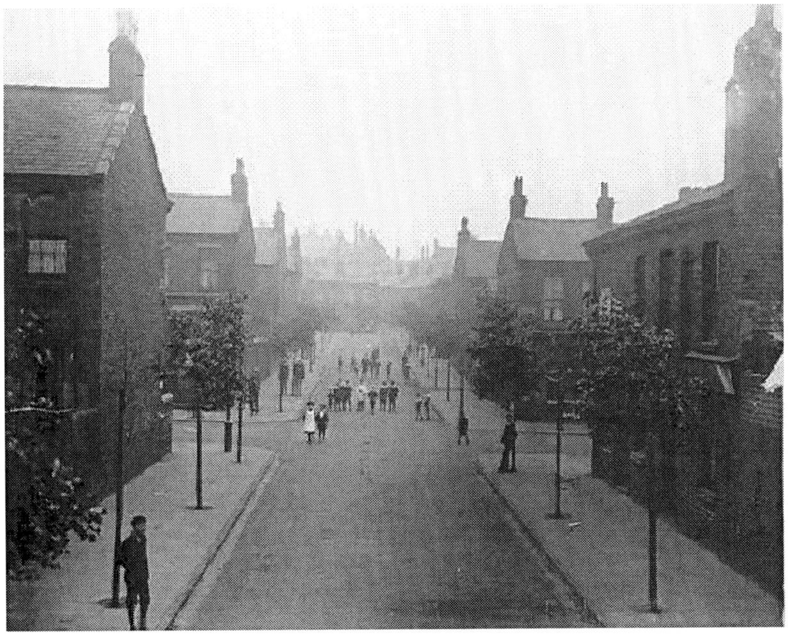

Dickens Street, July 1911 from Upper Warwick Street looking towards Northumberland Street. This scene looks remarkably similar today.

Sussex Gardens were therefore afforded some of the more modern designs of these smaller blocks, most notably the entrances and stairwells. Part of this tenement development still exists as Acorn Court. Facing these flats across Upper Warwick Street are a number of themed streets. Dickens Street ran to Northumberland Street, off which are streets named after characters created by Dickens. Pickwick, Dombey, Dorrit, Nickleby, Copperfield, Micawber, Pecksniff and Weller Street refer.

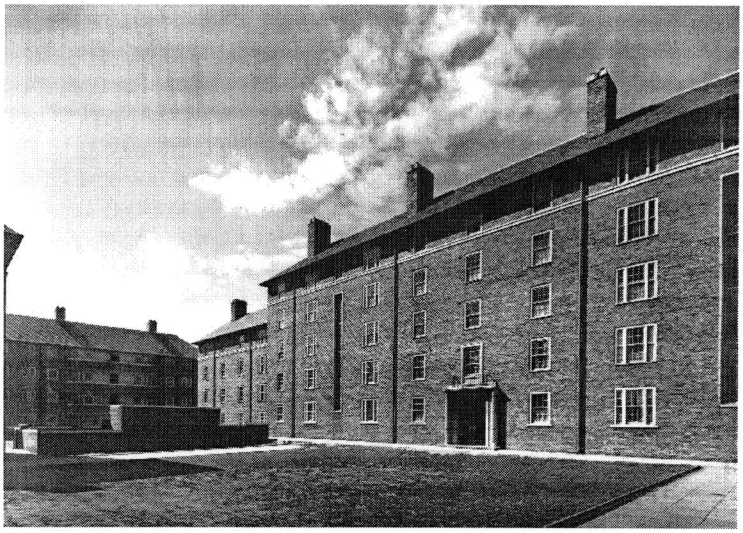

Sussex Gardens, newly completed in 1950

Across Windsor Street just to their east are streets named after characters created by Tennyson. These are Gwendoline, Geraint, Enid, Elaine, Merlin, Maud, Shallot, Madelaine and Claribel Street. Mill Street which was originally Bedford Street is named after the mill which stood at its junction with Hill Street though many other mills stood along its length, giving rise to the areas nickname as 'Little Holland'. Spillers Mill still exists on Mill Street, bounded by Corn, Bran and Grain Street. King Gardens, a post war tenement development from 1949 was constructed due to the chronic housing shortage immediately after the war. Some of the blocks contained a more modern vertical glass skylight to the stairwells. The Grapes Public House, more recently existing as the Dick Jennings though it is now derelict, is listed as 55 Mill Street. This stands on the corner of Hill Street and Mill Street and once separating the blocks of King Gardens.

They were amongst some of the shortest lived tenements, lasting less than 40 years before demolition in 1988. Mersey Parks Residential and

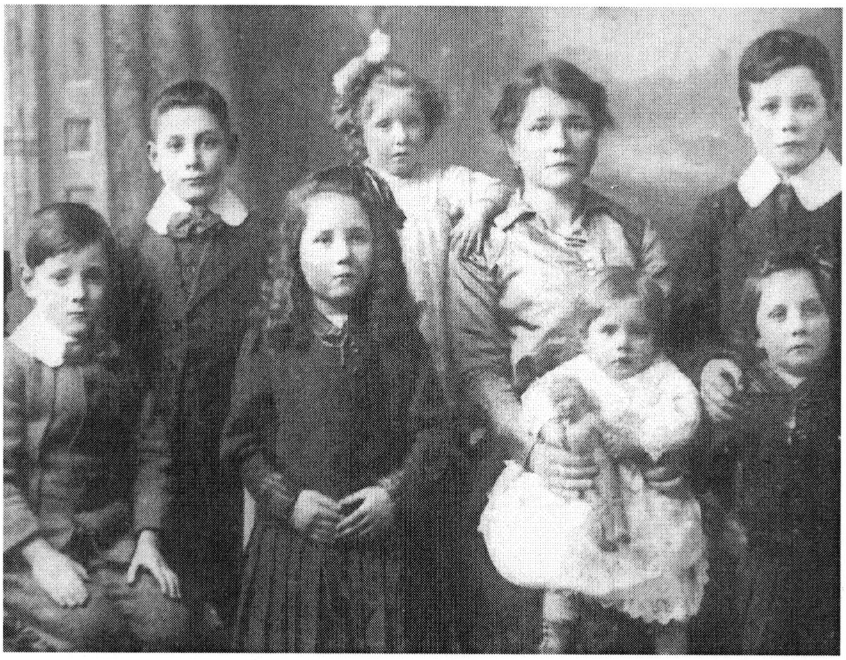

The Grealey family who when this was taken c1915 were living in Wolfe Street, Dingle. Pictured with their mother Catherine are (back row) Thomas, Rose (known as Dot) who is my father-in-law's mother and John. (front row) Michael, May, William and Florence. The man of the house John was away at sea serving in the 1st World War at the time. Catherine was to die just 3 years after this photograph was taken.

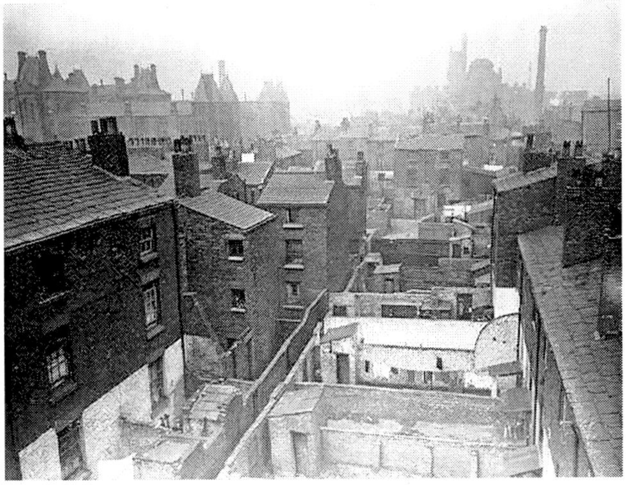

Nursing Home for the elderly is now situated on this site. A well known part of Dingle is known as the Holy Land which are four streets off Mill Street, namely David, Jacob, Isaac and Moses.

Sandwiched between Upper Parliament Street and Upper Stanhope Street is Chesterfield Street. St. James church, built to its West Side in 1775 is one of the oldest surviving church structures in the city. It fronts onto St. James Place and its cemetery is to be found in the sunken grounds of the Anglican

A 1934 rooftops scene of the rears of Grafton Street and Upper Mann Street showing squalor and dilapidation. The Royal Southern Hospital is on the skyline to the left whilst the Higsons brewery, now Cains, is on the right.

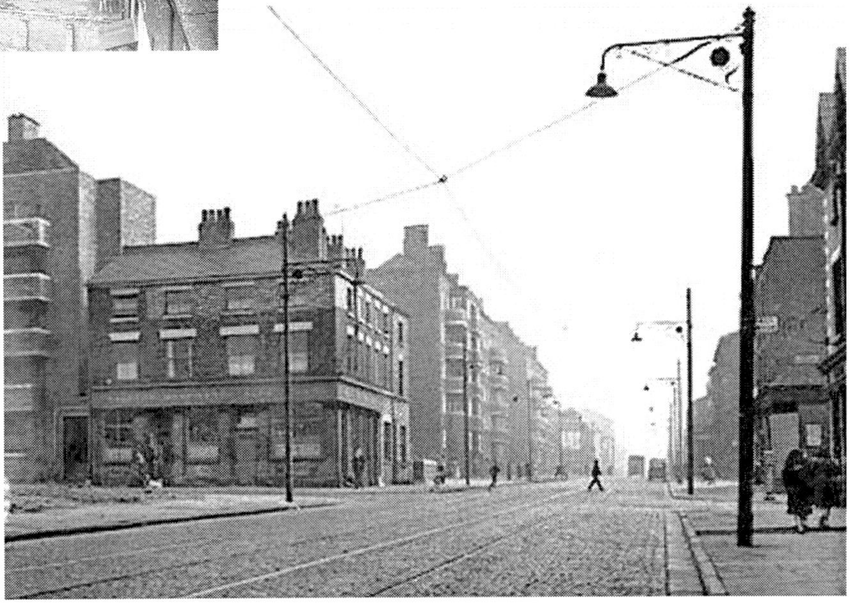

King Gardens in 1952 seen here either side of the Grapes Public House on the junction of Mill Street and Hill Street. The pub is now disused, last known as the Dick Jennings after its last landlord.

August 1954 and this is King Gardens courtyard on Mill Street.

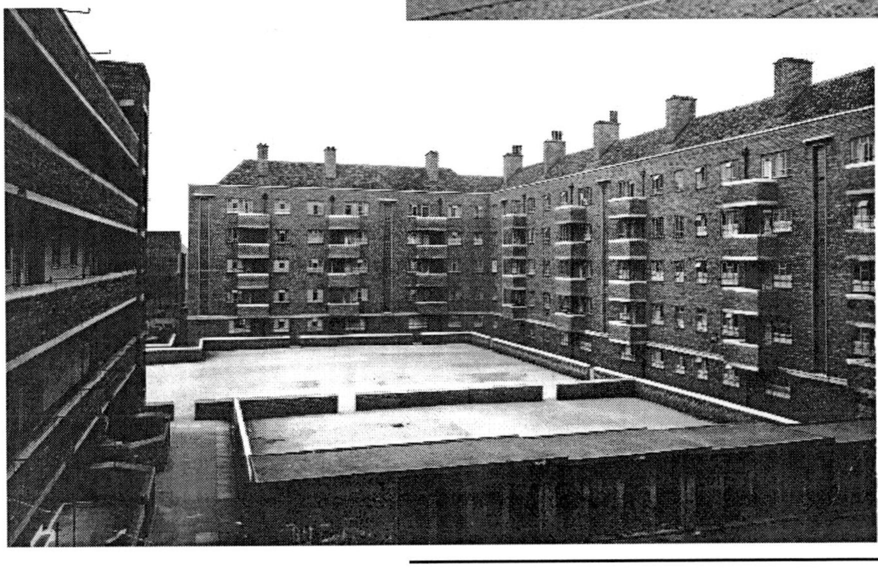

Cathedral. The East side of Chesterfield Street contained early slum terracing dating from the 1820s when it replaced Spring Gardens.

On its junction with Upper Stanhope Street stood the Chesterfield Arms Public House whose last licensee throughout the 1930s was a Bernard Caffrey. The block in question was demolished in

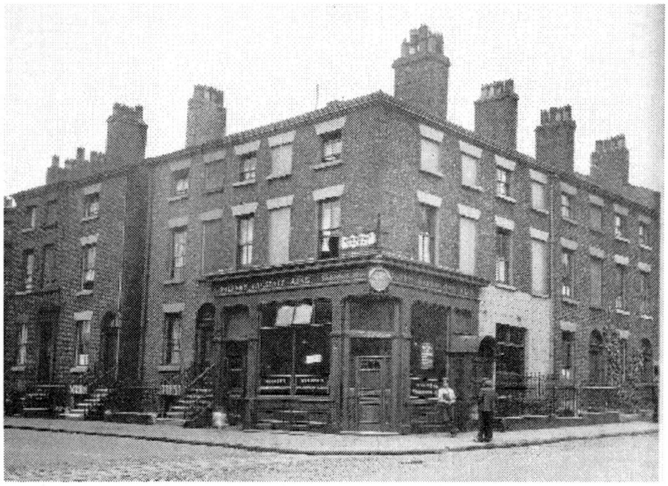

The Chesterfield Public House in 1934 just before this corner was demolished for the building of Stanhope House tenements.

1937 whereupon Stanhope House was built and opened a year later. Forming a 'c' shape, it contained 68 flats built over five storeys. Its main arched entrance was in a central recessed block with small side gardens on Upper Stanhope Street with a further arch in each of its other projections on Chesterfield Street and Blair Street. The blocks took their name from the street on which it was built which was the continuation of Stanhope Street.

Stanhope was the surname of the Earl of Harrington, the name by which the area was once known. Although derelict from the late 1980s, the blocks were not demolished until the mid 1990s when new flats were built on their site.

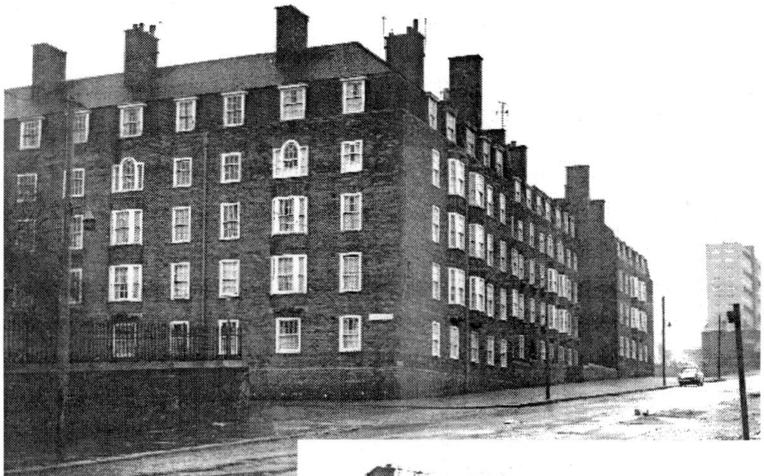

The same shot in 1975 showing the tenements.

The small tract of land to the east of Park Lane and St. James Street was home to four separate tenement developments. There are a number of thoroughfares preceded by the word Park in this Liverpool 1 and 8 area of the city. Park Lane, Park Road, Park Street, High Park Street etc are all derived as being the main routes which led to Toxteth Park.

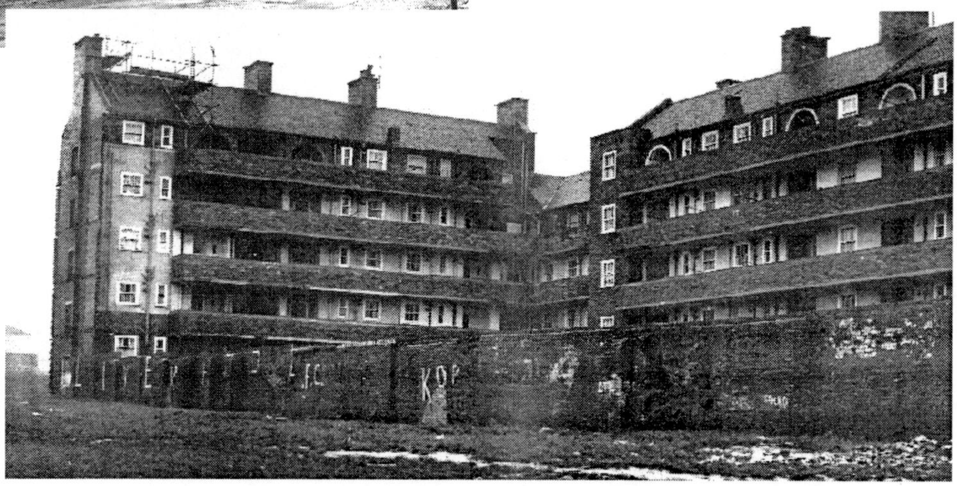

Another 1975 view of Stanhope House from Upper Parly. The local Kopites have been very busy with the white gloss paint.

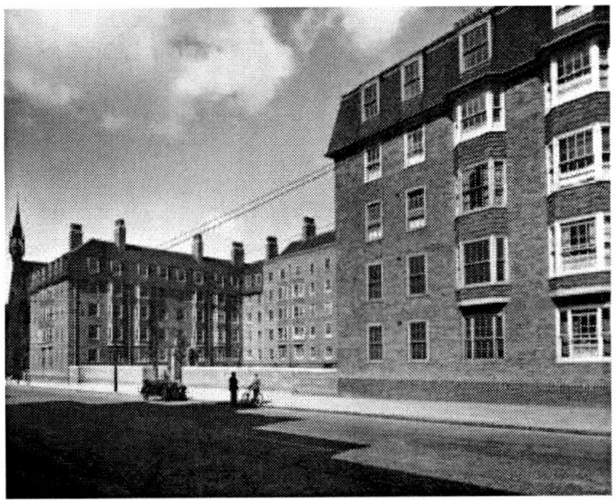

Prince Albert Gardens on St. James Street. This view is looking towards the city centre and St. Vincent De Paul Church which dates from 1852 and still stands today.

Prince Albert Gardens were built on the same block and adjacent to St. Vincent De Paul RC Church, fronting onto St. James Street and bordered by Hardy Street, Upper Frederick Street and Duncan Street. The middle block was set back from the road with a walled garden either side of the main arched entrance, a feature of some of the blocks in this area. These tenements had replaced a densely populated slum area that had been in existence since the 1700s. The church is still there but the site of the block of flats is now taken up by new housing on a new road layout called Prince Albert Mews in commemoration of the blocks that were named after Queen Victoria's cousin who was also her husband and Consort.

St. James Gardens were very similar in style to Prince Albert Gardens and were built to the north side of Hardy Street

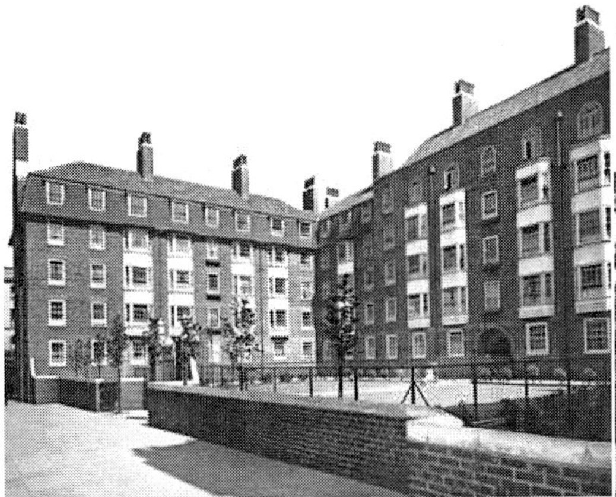

St. James Gardens entrance, courtyard and gardens as seen from St. James Street in 1935.

An aerial view showing St. James Gardens and Prince Albert Gardens in relation to the Anglican Cathedral.

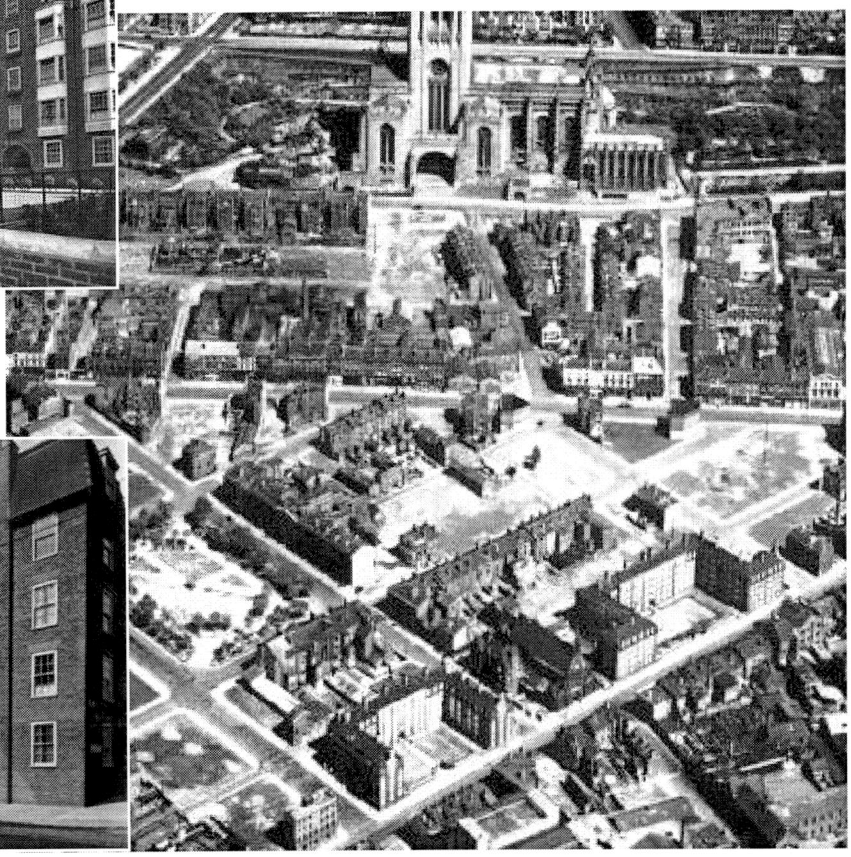

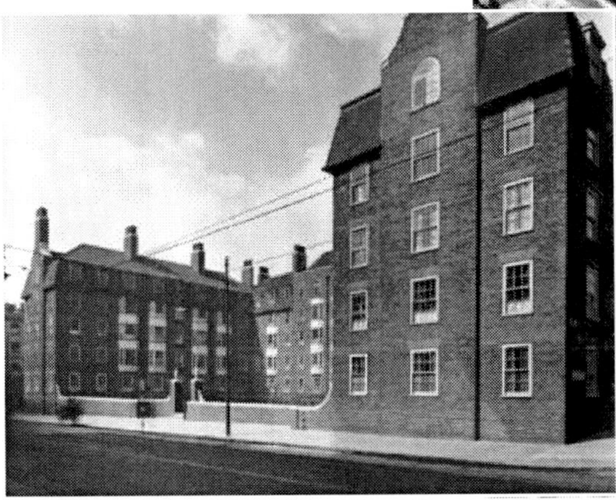

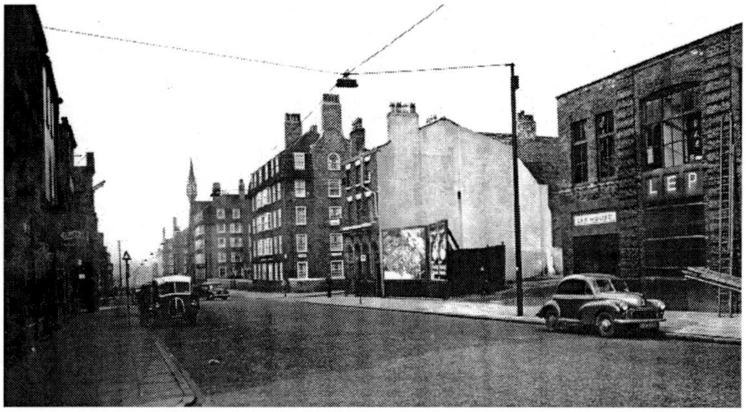

10/2/56. St. James Street looking past the Lep Transport offices and the tennies.

meaning that only St. Vincent De Paul Church separated these two blocks. Also hailing from 1935, they too had a recessed block with a main arched entrance set back from the road with gardens either side of its approach path. Like its near neighbours, the back elevation to these five storey blocks were broken from uniformity by the inclusion of bay windows at regular intervals. These blocks lasted until 1981.

This area is rich in having streets named after eminent people in Britain's history and local popular figures. Argyle Street is named after John, the Duke of Argyle who is celebrated by Sir Walter Scott in his work 'Heart of Midlothian'. Berry Street and Henry Street are in commemoration of Liverpool's 2nd dock engineer Henry Berry who lived on Duke Street whilst Cleveland Square is after John Cleveland. He was Liverpool's Mayor of 1703 and an MP for the Borough from 1710 until 1713.

25/9/37. Looking down St. James Street and Park Lane from the tower of St. James Church.

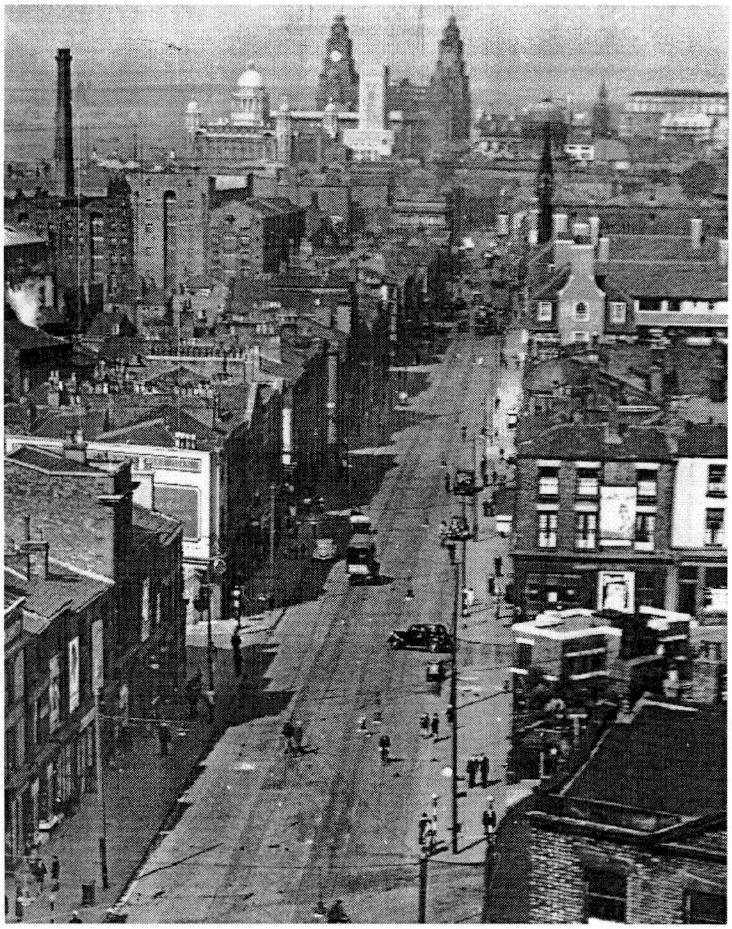

Cornwallis Street is called after Charles, the 1st Marquis Cornwallis who was Governor of Ireland and Governor General of India, responsible for negotiating the Peace of Amiens in 1802. Colquitt Street commemorates John Colquitt, a local landowner and collector of Customs and Excise duties. Frederick Street is after Frederick Louis, Prince of Wales who was the eldest son of King George II and father to King George III who himself had a square named after him nearby.

Hanover Street, originally King Street is named after the reigning Royal family from when it was re-laid and Kent Street takes the name of Richard Kent, a ship-owner and sea faring Merchant who possessed a mansion in this street. Lydia Ann Street took its name from the wife of George Perry, manager of the nearby Phoenix foundry where Merseyside's first marine engine was built. Parr Street, after Thomas Parr, was a local banker and owner of the mansion on Colquitt Street that became the Royal Institution.

Seel Street is named after local land and property owner Thomas Seel. He too was a merchant who had extensive gardens and a house in Hanover Street. Slater Street is in commemoration of Gill Slater who was the 1st Captain of the Liverpool Volunteer Corps who in 1766 were gathered to command when a French invasion was threatened. Wolstenholme Square was built on land owned by the family of the same name who had laid out the first ever enclosed garden in the city.

Nelson Street tenements in the heart of Chinatown. The ground floor is taken up by commercial premises that front onto Nelson Street, the street furniture being of a classical Chinese design. The inner courtyard is now a private car park for the residents

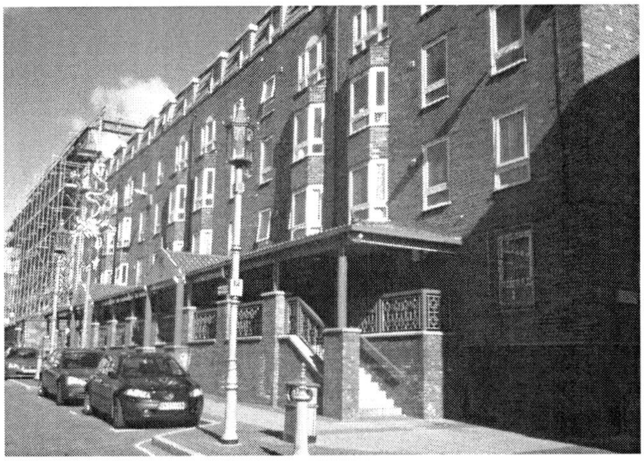

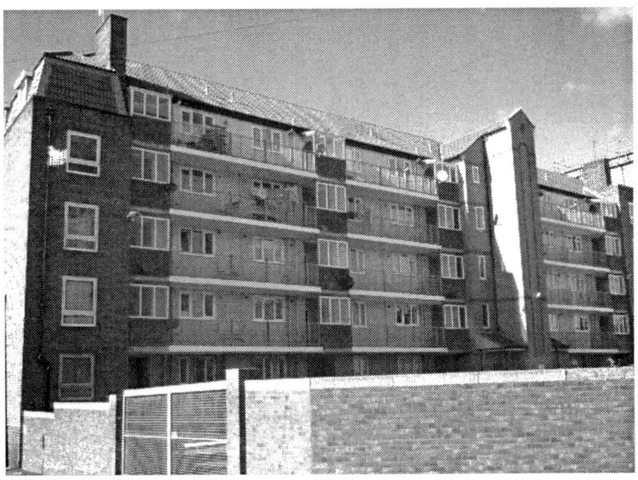

Pitt Street takes the name of William Pitt the Elder, the 1st Earl Chatham who was Prime Minister in 1756.Grenville Street South is after Lord Grenville who was Foreign Secretary to Pitt until taking over as PM from him upon his death. In 1807, Grenville introduced the Bill for the abolition of the slave trade. This street is unusual in being on its second name change. The macabre reason for its name change from Leveson Street is because in 1849 there was the quintuple murder of the pregnant wife of ships captain and later Liverpool dockmaster, John Hinrichson, their two children and their maid. Young Irishman Maurice Gleeson was found guilty and hung at Kirkdale Gaol in front of a large crowd. The street gained so much notoriety as for a change of name to be sanctioned. Almost as unusual is the fact that this street was originally Grenville Street in the first place, south was added even though there was no north.

The last surviving tenement block just south of the city centre is situated on Nelson Street. Constructed in the 1920s and containing just 25 flats, they are in the heart of Europe's oldest

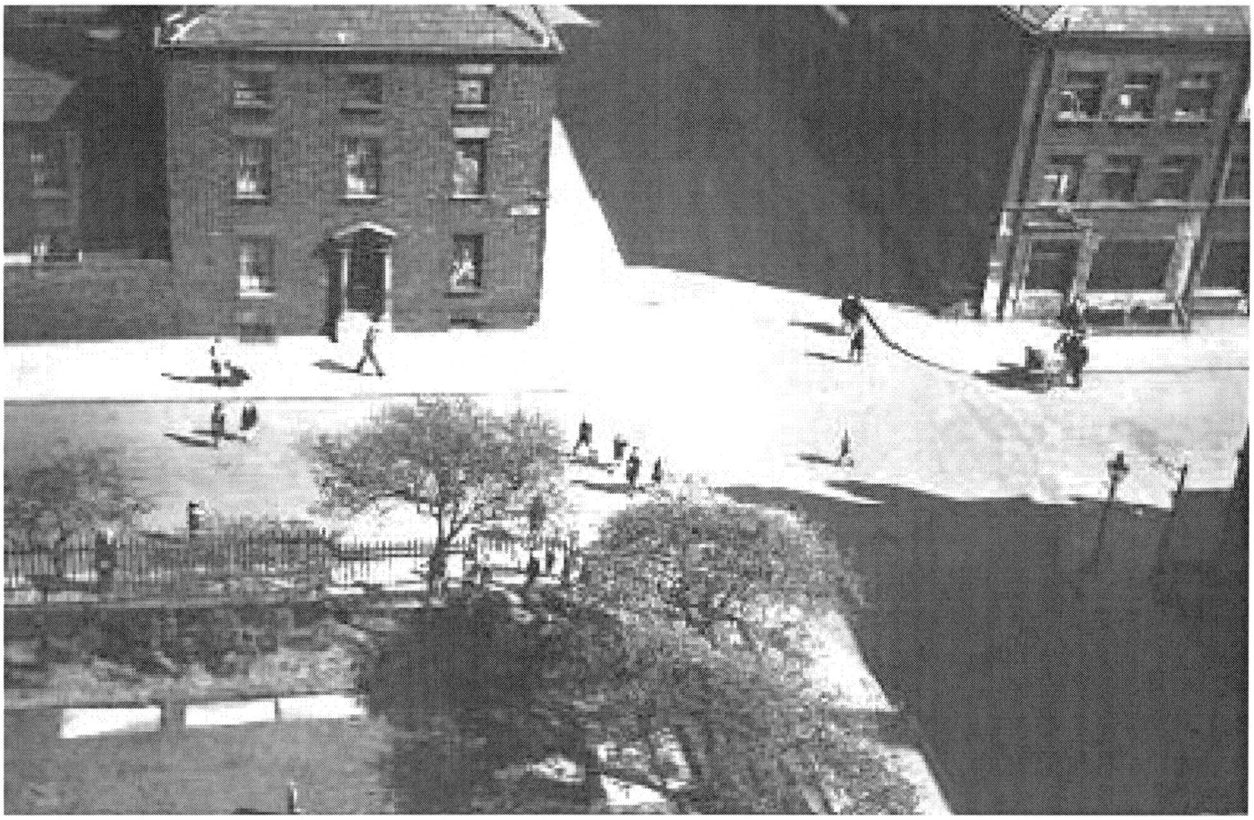

Taken from the top of St. Michael's Church. This is Cornwallis Street and Kent Street in all its Georgian splendour pre Kent Gardens tenements

Chinatown and face a line of Chinese Restaurants. They adjoin the 'Blackie' which was built in 1841 as a congregational Church. This architectural landmark within the city was converted in 1968 to the Great George Community Culture Project Centre. Nelson Street tenements have been restored to include a new central staircase and the small square which fronts it now serves as a car park for the residents. Nelson Street was laid out in the early 19th Century, named after national hero, Horatio.

Amazingly, prior to the slum dwellings that were encroaching ever more from the city's central area to what was rural Toxteth Park, this area was beautiful countryside. Laid out with gardens, springs and squares, the wealthy and distinguished such as William Roscoe chose this as their home. As an author, poet, artist, botanist, MP, lawyer and banker, Roscoe is no doubt one of Liverpool's most famous celebrated eminent gentlemen.

By the mid 1800s, many rows of established Georgian town houses had been erected around St. Michaels Church and its lush surrounding

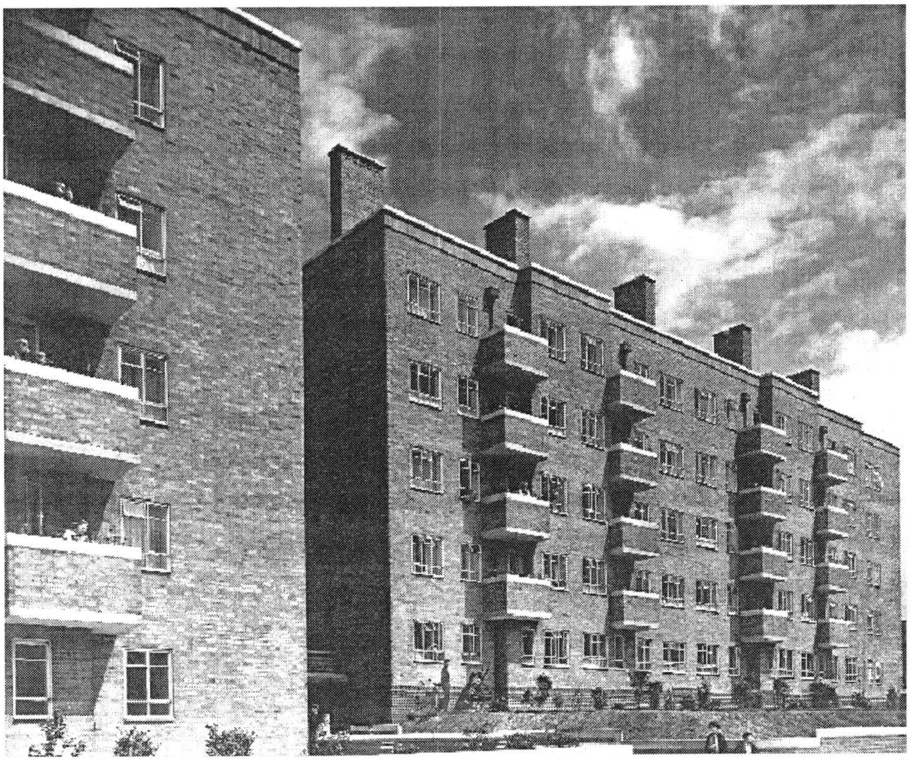

gardens. This magnificent Church, built in 1816 and consecrated a decade later housed ten 32 feet columns surmounted by a suitable entablature and pediment to its fine West portico. Indeed this piece of the structure was an identical copy of the Temple of Jupitor Stator in the forum in Rome. Kent Street, Cornwallis Street and Pitt Street were desirable addresses as an increasing number of merchants were fleeing the inner city desperation that was abound. Much of this area escaped the slum clearance programme of the early 1930s, but not the German Luftwaffe a decade later.

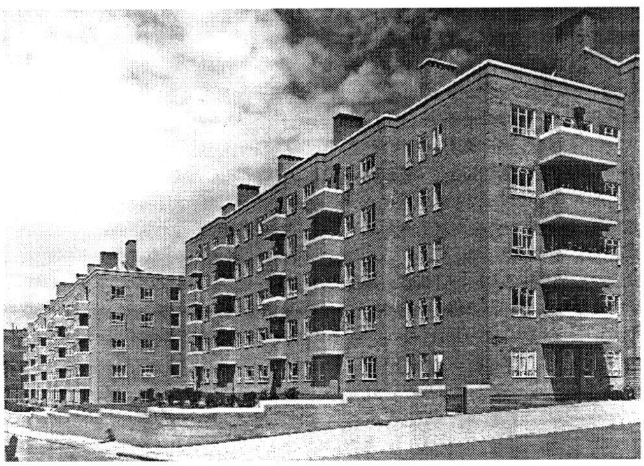

Kent Gardens nearing completion in May 1948. Seen here from a number of different angles, notably from Pitt Street and Suffolk Street.

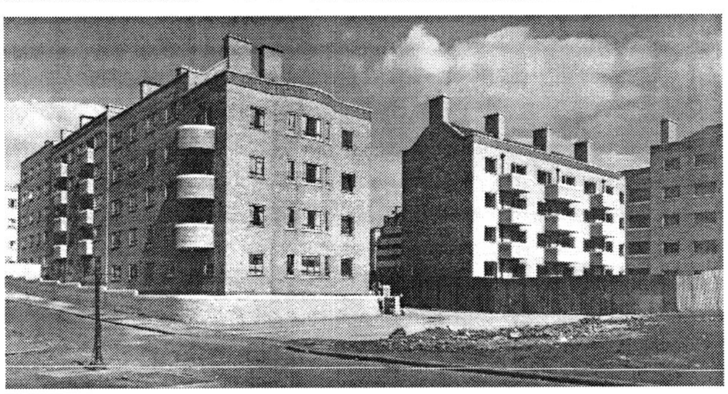

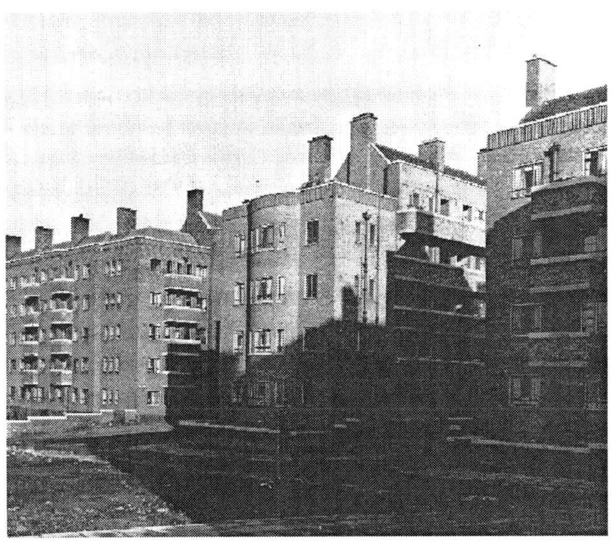

Shortly after the war, the dereliction was cleared and work was started on the construction of Kent Gardens which contained flats on Kent Street, Suffolk Street, Lydia Ann Street, Gilbert Street and Pitt Street. The blocks were set apart from each other with access roads, some of the blocks being four storeys with curved veranda's whilst most were 5 storeys with the standard oblong balconies. They were completed for habitation by 1948 but as with most of these tenement blocks that were a luxury unknown at the time, they themselves had fallen into a state of disrepair by the late 1980s. Befalling their own slum clearance programme, new housing with front and back gardens now saturate this area east of Park Lane almost to the fringes of the city centre behind Duke Street. Kent Street was for many years the City Council's gaslight and then electricity street lighting offices and depots known as City lighting which was also responsible for all street signs. Many of the long straight streets in this area were rope walks serving the ship building industry and chandlers for the yards that were so prevalent around the Kings Dock area.

With this sweep from north of the city, out to the East and swinging back in from the south, we have taken in all of the inter-war tenements and the few post war blocks that were built in the same style. As part of the city's housing history, if nothing else they formed communities that ex residents still talk about with much enthusiasm as they hark back to much friendlier, easier going and innocent times.

ACKNOWLEDGEMENTS

Thanks as ever to John, Jean and their team at Countyvise Publishing.

All copyright permissions have either be obtained or sought.

Other photographs of tenement developments can be found in similar books in this series:

In a city living ISBN 1 901231 51 8

In a city living 2 ISBN 1 901231 56 9

For some of the photographs featured in this book we have to thank individuals such as Harry Ainscough, Joe Devine, Brian Martin, Brian Saville, RJS Wiseman and Roger O'Hara for having the presence of mind to capture history in the making.

The following websites are fantastic sources of local information:

www.scottiepress.org
www.kirkdaleonline.co.uk
www.toxteth.net
www.dinglerenaissance.co.uk
www.liverpoolpictorial.co.uk
www.wavertreesociety.org
www.emanuensis.btinternet.co.uk
www.gardensofstone.mysite.wanadoo-members.co.uk
www.portcities.org.uk
www.mersey-gateway.org.uk/pastliverpool
www.liverpoolpictorial.co.uk/ainscough

I hope you have enjoyed reading this book.
Ged Fagan.